A Horace Reader

For Advanced Placement*

*AP and Advanced Placement Program are registered trademarks of the College Entrance Examination Board which was not involved in the production of this textbook, and does not endorse this product.

A Horace Reader
For Advanced Placement

Henry V. Bender, Ph.D.

Focus Publishing
R. Pullins Co.
Newburyport, MA
www.pullins.com

To
Dr. John C. Traupman
Emeritus, St. Joseph's University

ISBN 10: 0-941051-67-6
ISBN 13: 978-0-941051-67-5

Cover: Signorelli, Luca (1441-1523). Horace (Roman poet, 65-8 BCE). Fresco, 1500-1503. Post-restoration. Duomo, Orvieto, Italy. Scala/Art Resource, NY.

10 9 8 7 6 5

0507W

Contents

List of Illustrations

Preface

My intention in writing this book is to provide students of Latin with a relatively easy access to the poetry of Horace, which has often been considered difficult and remote. I wanted to make available a full assortment of Horace's poems which have been and are now the selections of the Educational Testing Service for the Advanced Placement Examination in Latin Literature.

Vocabulary has been supplied on the left page of the open book, as well as, when possible, below the Latin text which appears on the right page. Nouns are all listed with full nominative and full genitive case forms. Second-declension nouns whose stem ends in "i" are shown with a genitive singular "i(i)"; all third-declension adjectives with two terminations are listed with full forms separated by a dash; single terminations appear in nominative and genitive. The fourth part of a verb is always listed in a final "um". Standard abbreviations for gender, parts of speech, and number are used throughout. When a word is given in the vocabulary, only meanings that can work in the translation of the poem are supplied. The full vocabulary at the end of the text lists all vocabulary words supplied by the textbook. A brief introduction accompanies each poem. The print is 14 point, which allows for quicker and more comfortable study. There are more selections in the book than those required by the new A.P. syllabus, which justifies the title, *A Horace Reader*, and will afford the ambitious student the opportunity to read more than the A.P. requires.

I hope that students who use this textbook will read and understand Horace much more easily. A student's mastery of vocabulary and grammar should produce a smooth and clear translation of the Latin poem. The student should be able to translate the poem accurately in class without reference to any secondary material such as notes or an English translation. In order to obtain a complete understanding of each poem, a student should pay particular attention to any background material supplied in the notes.

Since the Advanced Placement examination does not use macrons, no attempt has been made to indicate long vowels. When this is a problem, the teacher's guidance is expected; a dictionary can always be consulted. Supplements include a chapter on meter and one on figures of speech. The student must understand that to learn anything effort must be put forth. Patience, consistency, and dedication will assure the student's success in the challenging but rewarding endeavor to read the poems of Horace.

To the study of Horace a student should bring three years of high school Latin, a compelling interest in ancient poetry, and some understanding of Roman history and culture. When an ode is assigned to the class, each student should practice reading the poem aloud in its meter. Attention needs to be paid to rhythm, scansion, and tonal variations, since meter was the music of the poet. The student should be able to recognize subtle figures of speech and to connect them with the more important question of developing the theme of the poem.

At the discretion of the teacher, students may have access to secondary literature (commentaries as well as in articles) to enhance their understanding of and response to the poems. In class, the testing of the poems should be thorough, reflecting a combination of grammar, syntax, identification, background, interpretation, and translation.

The student should be prepared to think about and to discuss the meaning of each poem. Ideally each poem should be studied as an entity in itself, and then be compared to its neighboring pieces (when this is possible). The poetry of Horace forms a magnificent mosaic composed of pieces of varying size and dimension. Each piece is a whole by itself, but acquires greater importance when placed in its proper setting in the whole.

It is a great achievement to be able to read Horace, as others before us have done, and to relate so much of what he has to say to the human condition which we all share.

Acknowledgments

This book began thirteen years ago in a sophomore classroom at St. Joseph's Preparatory School in Philadelphia, when I decided to teach a unit on Horace to a bright group of second year high school students. Since then, this book has evolved into an Advanced Placement textbook through many stages and is really the product of the years of suggestions and changes offered by my colleagues and students.

Early versions were used in area secondary schools by several teachers. I would like to extend my sincere gratitude to Michele Simon, Jeannette Keshishian, and Stephen Ciraolo of the Baldwin School, Brian Donaher and Paul Moynahan of the Boston College High School, Edward DeHoratius of The Bancroft School, Peter O' Sullivan of Xavier Academy, Connecticut., Carol Berardelli of North Penn High School, Molly Konopka of Episcopal Academy, Debby Lemieur of Gwynned Mercy Academy, Jonathan Rocky of Montgomery Christian Academy, and Dr. Dorothy Lange of Rutgers Preparatory School.

I am grateful to Professor Gregory Nagy of Harvard for his stimulating sessions on lyric poetry which have left their touch on this manual. Sessions with Dr. Lee Pearcy of the Episcopal Academy and Professor Matthew Santirocco of New York University, directors of an NEH Master Grant on Recovering Horace for the Curriculum, and with other seminar participants helped clarify many aspects of Horace's poetry.

This text would never have assumed the shape that it has without the generous scholarly direction lavished upon it by Professor John C. Traupman, emeritus from St. Joseph's University. Professor Traupman's familiarity with Horace is only outdone by his familiarity as a lexicographer with the intricacies of Latin syntax and vocabulary. The extent of my feelings of gratitude is indicated by the dedication.

To Ron Pullins of Focus Publishing goes a special accolade for his earnest patience. I owe a particular debt of gratitude to Stephen Ciraolo, for his friendship, encouragement and unfailing advice. While all attempts have been made to see that these textbooks are error free, all responsibility for errors remains with me.

> Henry V. Bender, Ph.D.
> June 1998
> The Hill School
> Chairman of Humanities
> and Adjunct Professor at
> Villanova University

TABLE OF IMPORTANT DATES

December 8, 65 B.C.	Birth of Horace in Venusia in Apulia
60 B.C.	First Triumvirate of Pompey, Caesar, Crassus
45 B.C. (perhaps)	Horace goes to Greece.
44 B.C.	Assassination of Julius Caesar; Horace joins forces of Brutus in Greece.
43 B.C.	Second triumvirate of Octavian, Antony, Lepidus; Horace becomes a military tribune.
42 B.C.	Battle of Philippi, in which Horace participates; defeat of the forces of Brutus and Cassius
41 B.C.	Horace is pardoned; becomes quaestorial secretary; begins to meet influential, educated Romans.
39-38 B.C.	Horace becomes a member of Maecenas' circle of poets.
35-34 B.C.	Satires Book I (10 poems) is published.
31 B.C.	Battle of Actium; Octavian defeats Marc Antony and Cleopatra.
30 B.C.	Horace publishes Satires Book II (8 poems), and Epodes (17 iambic poems).
27 B.C.	Senate gives the title *Augustus* to Octavian.
23 B.C.	Horace publishes Odes Books I, II, III (88 poems).
20-19 B.C.	Epistles Book I (20 letters in hexameters)
19 B.C.	Vergil dies.
17 B.C.	Carmen Saeculare (centennial song for the city of Rome)
13 B.C.	Horace publishes Odes Book IV (15 poems) and Epistles Book II *(Ars Poetica).*
October, 8 B.C.	Maecenas dies; November 27, 8 B.C., Horace dies.

On Horace

The lyric poet Quintus Horatius Flaccus was born on December 8 in 65 B.C. The place of his birth was Venusia in the province of Apulia in southeastern Italy. Substantial details of Horace's life can be found both in his various literary works and in a biographical tradition based upon the biography by the Latin author Suetonius (A.D. 70-140). Using these details we can reconstruct the life of Horace and further understand his poetry.

Horace's father was an ex-slave (in Latin *libertinus*) (*Satires* I.6.6, 45-6; Suetonius, *Vita Horati*). We do not know whether Horace's father came to Italy as a slave from the East, or whether he was a native Italian. By his own admission (*Satires* I.4.103-29), Horace received a traditional Italian up-bringing from a father who seems to have known the values and ways of the old world. Whether he was a an immigrant or a native, Horace's father seems not to have been respected, as Suetonius suggests in the following story.

> *Q. Horatius Flaccus, Venusianus, patre ut ipse tradit libertino et exactionum coactore (ut vero creditum est salsamentario, cum illi quidam in altercatione exprobrasset:"Quotiens ego vidi patrem tuum brac(c)hio se emungentem!")*

> Quintus Horatius Flaccus from Venusia, his father being an ex-slave, as he himself reports, and a collector of taxes (or, as in fact is believed, a dealer in salted fish, since someone in an altercation had reproached Horace, "How many times have I seen your father wiping his nose on his forearm!")

His father seems to have made enough money (*Satires* I.6.86) to finance an excellent education in Rome and Athens for Horace (*Satires* I.6.76-80; *Epistles* II.1.70f). According to Horace (*Satires* I.6.47f) while he was in Athens, Brutus made him a tribune, a high ranking army officer. This is confirmed by Suetonius:

> *bello Philippensi excitus a Marco Bruto imperatore, tribunus militum meruit*

> (Horace) was summoned to the war at Philippi by Marcus Brutus the commander, and served as a tribune of the soldiers.

In *Odes* II.14, Horace writes of his experience in that war and suggests how he was reconciled with the winner, Octavian. Of course, Horace seems to have had little military experience at all, and so it remains a question why he was promoted to such an important rank as tribune in the first place. The rank of tribune was usually reserved for the *equites,* the highest class of Romans below the senatorial class. At any rate, when Brutus and his army lost at Philippi in 42 B.C., Horace lost his fortune, including all his father's property. (*Satires* I.6.71; *Epistles* II.1.70f).

Eventually Horace returned to Italy, was pardoned and became a clerk for a quaestor, a treasury official in Rome, as the *Vita* confirms:

> *victisque partibus venia impetrata scriptum quaestorium comparavit.*

> When Brutus' party was defeated and forgiveness obtained, he acquired the position of quaestor's secretary.

We do not know how long Horace worked in this capacity, but we may assume that he began to develop new friendships which led him into the company of other educated literary figures.

The poetry that Horace (*Epistles* II.2.51f) composed at this time caught the attention of Maecenas, Octavian's powerful friend, who was charged with discovering competent poets and writers. Apparently in the 38 B.C., Maecenas introduced Horace to the literary circle which he had been forming (*Satires* I.6.52-62; II.6.40-42). Horace refers to the Sabine farm which Maecenas secured for him in 36 B.C. Owning such a property alleviated his financial worries and allowed Horace to write. He made many friends and was well known and well accepted by a wide variety of Romans. He was extraordinarily close to his patron Maecenas, to whom he dedicated the first poem in *Satires, Epistles, and Odes*. Suetonius quotes an epigram of Maecenas addressed to Horace which corroborates their closeness:

> *Ni te visceribus meis, Horati,*
> *Plus iam diligo, tu tuum sodalem*
> *Ninnio videas strigosiorem.*

> If I do not love you now, Horace,
> more than my own next of kin, you
> would see your companion thinner
> than Ninnius.

Maecenas writes that Horace nourishes and sustains his life and that without Horace in his life, he would waste away.

There is literary evidence that Octavian (Augustus) and Horace had a good relationship as well. Augustus tried to employ Horace as his personal secretary. Suetonius refers to this by quoting a letter of Augustus written to Maecenas:

> *Augustus epistolarum quoque ei officium optulit, ut hoc ad Maecenatem scripto significat: "Ante ipse sufficiebam scribendis epistulis amicorum, nunc occupatissimus et infirmus Horatium nostrum a te cupio abducere. Veniet ergo ab ista parasitica mensa ad hanc regiam, et nos in epistulis scribendis iuvabit."*

Augustus also offered Horace the position of personal secretary, as he makes clear in this letter written to Maecenas: "Formerly I myself was up to writing letters to my friends; now I am extremely busy and unhealthy and I want to take our Horace from you. Therefore he will come from that parasitic table to this palatial one, and will help us in writing letters."

Horace refused the invitation but still enjoyed the emperor's good will. Augustus was convinced that Horace's poetry was immortal. Just after the battle of Actium in 31 B.C., Horace published a collection of seventeen poems, modeled on those of the Greek lyric poet Archilochus. These were called *Epodes* or *Iambi*. Traditionally, such compositions conveyed hostile criticism or sarcastic invective, and Horace's *Epodes* were no different. They reveal a care of composition and a sense of detail which will become characteristics of Horatian style.

At about the same time, Horace wrote the first of his two books of hexameter poetry, the *Satires* or *Sermones*. Book I contains ten satires. The fifth satire describes a journey to the town of Brundisium. Scholars believe that this trip happened in 38 B.C. and involved key members of the group of talented writers whom Maecenas was assembling. There are eight poems in Book II. The tone, occasions, and themes of both books of Satires demonstrate the versatility and skill of Horace. This textbook includes Satire I.9, which embodies all the characteristics of his style, including his wittiness, his meticulous choice of words, his extensive use of figures of speech, his irony, and, in this example, his humor.

Horace modeled his satires on those of the Roman satirist Lucilius (168-102 B.C.). It was Horace's intention to produce satires which would be more finished, better organized, and less overtly sarcastic than those of Lucilius. He also wanted his poems to illustrate the precision of words associated with the Greek lyric poet Callimachus (circa 270 B.C.). Book I of the Satires contains ten poems. The first nine can be divided into three groups of three, and the final tenth seems to be the poet's assessment of his work in poems 1-9. Sarcasm brings to mind Lucilius' style in satires 1-3; references to his own personal life and experiences connect satires 4-6; satires 7-9 seem "anecdotal" since their topics range from witches (7), to a statue of the god Priapus in a burial ground for paupers (8), to an impromptu encounter with an extremely talkative bore (9).

The eight satires in Book II are more integrated with one another. The first four poems parallel in some ways the second four. Satire 1 shows the poet asking for advice as a satirist; satire 5 as a person in need of help to recover his lost fortune; satires 2 and 6 deal with the value of the simple life; satires 3 and 7 show Horace receiving intense lectures from Stoic philosophers; satires 4 and 8 contain comments on excess in Roman banqueting. This kind of subtle arrangement and pattern of thematic unity will be seen in the *Odes*.

In 23 B.C., Horace published the first three books of his *Odes*. These poems, modeled on the poetry of Alcaeus, Sappho, and other archaic Greek lyricists, constitute a serious collection of ingenious commentary on many subjects such as love, politics and war, the mutability of life, the inevitability of death, and eagerness for challenge. After these lyric poems, Horace wrote the hexameters which became Book I of the *Epistles* in 20-19 B.C. On June 3, 17 B.C., Horace's *Carmen Saeculare,* a poem for Rome's centennial celebration, was sung. In 13 B.C., upon the demand of Augustus, a fourth book of odes appeared, as most probably did Book II of the *Epistles,* Horace's final work. Five years later in 8 B.C., Maecenas died. Only two months later, on November 27, Horace passed away leaving his entire estate to his declared heir, Augustus.

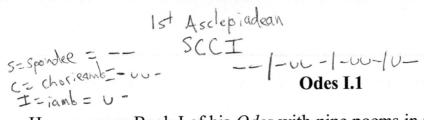

(handwritten annotations at top:)

1st Asclepiadean

SCCI

S = spondee = − −
C = choriamb = − ∪ ∪ −
I = iamb = ∪ −

− − | − ∪ ∪ − | − ∪ ∪ | ∪ −

Odes I.1

Horace opens Book I of his *Odes* with nine poems in nine different meters, rightly called Horace's "Parade Odes." Poem 10 repeats the Sapphic meter first seen in *Odes* I.2; poem 11 is in yet another meter. This first ode, dedicated to Horace's patron Maecenas, extols the role of the poet as an activity which is divine, as it enumerates other occupations which pale in comparison. The meter is first Asclepiadean.

Maecenas atavis edite regibus,   *(handwritten: PPP or prospet... PPl vocda)*
   O et praesidium et dulce decus meum,
(handwritten: diminutive) sunt quos curriculo pulverem Olympicum
   collegisse iuvat, metaque fervidis   *(handwritten: nom subj)*
evitata rotis palmaque nobilis   5
   terrarum dominos evehit ad deos;

(handwritten: 1st   2nd   4th/Alcaic   5th with underline markings)

1   **Maecenas: Maecenas, Maecenatis,** *m.,* Maecenas, friend and patron of Horace
    atavis: atavus, -a, -um, *adj.,* ancestral
    edite: editus, -a, -um, *adj.,* sprung from

2   Note that there is a hiatus between *O* and *et.*
    praesidium: praesidium, praesidi(i), *n.,* protection; protector
    decus: decus, decoris, *n.,* glory

3   **curriculo: curriculum, curriculi,** *n.,* racing chariot; a diminutive form from
        currus; a little chariot in the biggest of all races, the Olympic games
    pulverem: pulvis, pulveris, *m.,* dust

4   **collegisse: colligo, colligere, collegi, collectum,** collect, gather
    iuvat: iuvo, iuvare, iuvi, iutum, please, delight
    meta: meta, metae, *f.,* a stone turning post in a chariot race; *metae* were positioned
        at each end of the *spina,* the elevated center of the arena.
    fervidis: fervidus, -a, -um, *adj.,* glowing

5   **evitata: evito, evitare, evitavi, evitatum,** miss narrowly, graze
    rotis: rota, rotae, *f.,* wheel
    palmaque: palma, palmae, *f.,* palm branch; a wreath of wild olive was the prize
        at Olympia but a branch of palm was also carried by the winners in all of the
        games, a custom adopted by the Romans around 290 B.C.

6   **dominos,** in apposition with *quos* (line 3) retained as the object of *evehit*
    evehit: eveho, evehere, evexi, evectum, raise up

1

7   **hunc** (like **illum** in line 9): the direct objects of the understood verbs *iuvat* and *evehit*

   Quiritium: Quiris, Quiritis, *m.,* Roman citizen; the word makes associations with Quirinus, a name of the deified Romulus, founder of the Quirites, the descendants of Romulus

   mobilium: mobilis-mobile, *adj.,* fickle

8   **certat: certo, certare, certavi, certatum,** vie; compete

   tergeminis: tergeminus, -a, -um, *adj.,* triple; the triple offices of the *cursus honorum,* the political ladder: aedile, praetor, consul

   tollere: tollo, tollere, sustuli, sublatum, elevate, raise

9   **proprio: proprius, -a, -um,** *adj.,* one's own

   condere: condo, condere, condidi, conditum, store up

   horreo: horreum, horrei, *n.,* barn, granary

10   **Libyci:, Libycus, -a, -um,** *adj.,* Libyan, African; Libya was an important source of grain which was shipped to Rome for sale and distribution.

   verritur: verro, verrere, verri, versum, sweep

   areis: area, areae, *f.,* threshing floor

11   **gaudentem: gaudeo, gaudere, gavisus sum,** rejoice, take delight in

   findere: findo, findere, fidi, fissum, cleave, split

   sarculo: sarculum, sarculi, *n.,* hoe

12   **Attalicis: Attalicus, -a, -um,** *adj.,* of Attalus; the wealthy Pergamene king, Attalus III, who gave his kingdom to the Romans in 133B.C.

   condicionibus: condicio, condicionis, *f.,* term, condition; "terms that only an Attalus could offer."

13   **dimoveas: dimoveo, dimovere, dimovi, dimotum,** remove

   trabe: trabs, trabis, *f.,* beam, (by metonymy) ship

   Cypria: Cyprius, -a, -um, *adj.,* of the island of Cyprus, well known for shipbuilding

14   **Myrtoum: Myrtous, -a, -um,** *adj.,* Myrtoan; pertaining to the western part of the Aegean sea below the island of Euboea, the sea between the Peloponnesus and the Cyclades

   pavidus: pavidus, -a, -um, *adj.,* frightened, terrified

   secet: seco, secare, secui, sectum, cut

15   **luctantem: luctor, luctari, luctatus sum,** wrestle

   Icariis: Icarius, -a, -um, *adj.,* Icarian; the eastern Aegean Sea between the island Patmos and modern Turkey

   fluctibus: fluctus, fluctus, *m.,* wave; dative with the participle *luctantem*

   Africum: Africus, Africi, *m.,* the southwest wind

hunc, si mobilium turba Quiritium
certat tergeminis tollere honoribus;
illum, si proprio condidit horreo
quidquid de Libycis verritur areis.   10
gaudentem patrios findere sarculo
agros Attalicis condicionibus
numquam dimoveas ut trabe Cypria
Myrtoum pavidus nauta secet mare.
luctantem Icariis fluctibus Africum   15
mercator metuens otium et oppidi
laudat rura sui; mox reficit ratis
quassas, indocilis pauperiem pati.
est qui nec veteris pocula Massici
nec partem solido demere de die   20
spernit, nunc viridi membra sub arbuto

16 **mercator: mercator, mercatoris,** *m.,* merchant
    metuens: metuo, metuere, metui, fear
    otium: otium, oti(i), *n.,* leisure time, as opposed to business time *negotium*

17 **rura: rus, ruris,** *n.,* fields
    reficit: reficio, reficere, refeci, refectum, repair
    ratis: ratis, ratis, *f.,* ship

18 **quassas: quatio, quatere,** (no perfect active), **quassum,** shatter
    indocilis: indocilis-indocile, *adj.,* difficult to be taught
    pauperie: pauperies, pauperiei, *f.,* poverty
    pati: patior, pati, passus sum, endure

19 **pocula: poculum, poculi,** *n.,* cup
    Massici: Massicus, -a, -um, *adj.,* Massican; a noted wine from northern
       Campania

20 **demere: demo, demere, dempsi, demptum,** take away
    solido...de die, the "solid" day, the business day, the entire day

21 **spernit: sperno, spernere, sprevi, spretum,** scorn
    viridi: viridis-viride, *adj.,* green, fresh
    arbuto: arbutus, arbuti, *f.,* strawberry tree
    membra: membrum, membri, *n.,* body part, limb; body (accusative of respect)

22 **stratus: sterno, sternere, stravi, stratum,** spread, stretch
lene: lenis-lene, *adj.,* gentle, light
caput: caput, capitis *n.,* head, source

23 **lituo: lituus, litui,** *m.,* cavalry trumpet
tubae: tuba, tubae, *f.,* infantry trumpet

24 **permixtus: permisceo, permiscere, permiscui, permixtum,** mix, blend
sonitus: sonitus, sonitus, *m.,* sound

25 **detestata: detestor, detestari, detestatus sum,** detest
Iove: Iuppiter, Iovis, *m.,* Jupiter; (figuratively) sky

26 **venator: venator, venatoris,** *m.,* hunter
tenera: tener-tenera-tenerum, *adj.,* young, weak, tender

27 **catulis: catulus, catuli,** *m.,* puppy; hunting hound
cerva: cerva, cervae, *f.,* deer

28 **rupit: rumpo, rumpere, rupi, ruptum,** break
teretes: teres, teretis, *adj.,* thick, close meshed
Marsus: Marsus, -a, -um, *adj.,* Marsian, of or pertaining to a mountainous area in central Italy east of Rome noted for hunting and the tough soldiers it produced
aper: aper, apri, *m.,* wild boar
plagas: plaga, plagae, *f.,* net

29 Note the position of the pronoun *me*; this dramatically indicates the transition in the poem from the pursuits of other men to that of Horace's ambitions
doctarum: doctus, -a, -um, *adj.,* learned
hederae: hedera, hederae, *f.,* ivy, sacred to Bacchus, a god of inspiration and therefore the symbol of poets
frontium: frons, frontis, *f.,* brow

30 **gelidum: gelidus, -a, -um,** *adj.,* chilly, cold
nemus: nemus, nemoris, *n.,* grove

31 **Satyris: Satyrus, Satyri,** *m.,* Satyr, a forest deity with goat's feet, resembling an ape, frequent companion of Bacchus
chori: chorus, chori, *m.,* dance
levis: levis-leve, *adj.,* light-footed, lightly tripping

32 **secernunt: secerno, secernere, secrevi, secretum,** set apart
tibias: tibia, tibiae, *f.,* flute

stratus, nunc ad aquae lene caput sacrae.

multos castra iuvant et lituo tubae

permixtus sonitus bellaque matribus

detestata. manet sub Iove frigido   25

venator tenerae coniugis immemor,

seu visa est catulis cerva fidelibus,

seu rupit teretes Marsus aper plagas.

me doctarum hederae praemia frontium

dis miscent superis, me gelidum nemus   30

nympharumque leves cum Satyris chori

secernunt populo, si neque tibias

Euterpe cohibet nec Polyhymnia

Lesboum refugit tendere barbiton.

quodsi me lyricis vatibus inseres,   35

sublimi feriam sidera vertice.

[marginal handwritten notes:]
gen, ... poss
abl accomp
abl MW
word order
immemor coniugis is actually under cold Jupiter
OR
deer is surrounder by hounds
OR
boar is actually surrounded by twisted + nets
gen, dat, nom
pres act inf compl

33 Euterpe is the muse of lyric poetry; Polyhymnia the muse of religious song; together
they stand for all forms of lyric poetry.
cohibet: cohibeo, cohibere, cohibui, hold, hold back; "fails to play"

34 **Lesboum: Lesbous, -a, -um,** *adj.,* Lesbian; dealing with the island of Lesbos;
association with Sappho and lyric poetry is intended.
refugit tendere: "recoil from stretching"
barbiton: barbitos, barbiti, *m.,* lyre; the accusative singular is *barbiton.*

35 **quodsi: quodsi,** *conj.,* but if
vatibus: vates, vatis, *m.,* poet
inseres: insero, inserere, inserui, insertum, insert, place among

36 **sublimi: sublimis-sublime,** *adj.,* raised up, held high
feriam: ferio, ferire, strike
vertice: vertex, verticis, *m.,* the top of the head, head

Odes I.3

1   Normally the occurence of *sic* with an understood verb is followed by a subjunctive in a substantive clause introduced by *ut.* Here Horace uses the iussive subjunctive in *regat, reddas* and *serves.*
diva: diva, divae, *f.,* goddess
potens: potens, potentis, *adj.,* powerful
Cypri: Cyprus, Cypri, *f.,* island of Cyprus, haunt of Venus, thought to be the spot where the goddess first touched land after her birth from the sea

2   **Helenae: Helena, Helenae,** *f.,* Helen of Troy
fratres refers to the twin stars *(gemini),* Castor and Pollux, celestial points from which sailors at sea would take their bearing
lucida: lucidus, -a, -um, *adj.,* shining

3   **regat: rego, regere, rexi, rectum,** guide

4   **obstrictis: obstringo, obstringere, obstrinxi, obstrictum,** bind up, confine
Iapyga: Iapyx, Iapygis, *m.,* the wind which blew from Apulia, the southeastern section of Italy, to Greece; the wind is named from Iapyx, one of the lesser known sons of Daedalus.

6   **Atticis: Atticus, -a, -um,** *adj.,* Attic, Greek

7   **reddas: reddo, reddere, reddidi, redditum,** return
incolumem: incolumis-incolume, *adj.,* unharmed
precor: precor, precari, precatus sum, pray, beg

8   **animae: anima, animae,** *f.,* soul
dimidium: dimidium, dimidi(i), *n.,* half

9   **illi = illius**; Latin frequently uses a dative when English would use a possessive, especially with the body or parts thereof or the mind.
robur: robur, roboris, *n.,* oak
aes: aes, aeris, *n.,* bronze
triplex: triplex, triplicis, *adj.,* three-ply

10   **erat:** Horace frequently uses a singular verb with two or more subjects.
pectus: pectus, pectoris, *n.,* chest
fragilem: fragilis-fragile, *adj.,* fragile
truci: trux, trucis, *adj.,* fierce, angry (sea)

11   **commisit: committo, committere, commisi, commissum,** commit; entrust
pelago: pelagus, pelagi, *n.,* sea
ratem: ratis, ratis, *f.,* boat, ship

12   **praecipitem: praeceps, praecipitis,** *adj.,* headfirst, stormy
Africum: Africus, Africi, *m.,* southwest wind

This poem is addressed to the ship which is carrying Vergil on a voyage from Italy to Greece. Horace expresses his concern for Vergil's safety and then offers a meditation on why the reach of any human being beyond set limitations invites peril at every turn. This type of well-wishing send-off poem is called a *propemptikon*. Implicit in the poem may be a subtle caution to Vergil as he undertakes the composition of the *Aeneid*. The meter is second Asclepiadean .

Sic te diva potens Cypri,
sic fratres Helenae, lucida sidera,
   ventorumque regat pater
obstrictis aliis praeter Iapyga,
   navis, quae tibi creditum   5
debes Vergilium, finibus Atticis
   reddas incolumem precor,
et serves animae dimidium meae.
   illi robur et aes triplex
circa pectus erat, qui fragilem truci   10
   commisit pelago ratem
primus, nec timuit praecipitem Africum
   decertantem Aquilonibus
nec tristis Hyadas nec rabiem Noti,
   quo non arbiter Hadriae   15

13 **decertantem: decerto, decertare, decertavi, decertatum,** struggle; Horace frequently makes this verb govern the dative case.
   Aquilonibus: Aquilo, Aquilonis, *m.,* north wind; the noun is in the dative case governed by a verb of contending.

14 **Hyadas: Hyades, Hyadum,** *f.,* Hyades; rain stars whose setting in the morning and rising in the evening heralded the approach of storms
   tristis: tristis-triste, *adj.,* sad, gloomy, "rainy"
   rabiem: rabies, rabiei, *f.,* fury, rage
   Noti: Notus, Noti, *m.,* the south wind

15 **quo,** ablative of comparison
   arbiter: arbiter, arbitri, *m.,* controller, lord
   Hadriae: Hadria, Hadriae, *f.,* the Adriatic Sea

16 **maior:** suply *est.*
    tollere: tollo, tollere, sustuli, sublatum, raise
    seu: the first *seu* is omitted, as often in poetry: *seu tollere seu ponere*
    ponere: pono, ponere, posui, positum, put down, calm
    vult, third singular present indicative active from *volo, velle, volui,* wish, want
    freta: fretum, freti, *n.,* straight, (figuratively) waves; recalls *fluctus.*

17 **gradum: gradus, gradus,** *m.,* step, approach

18 **siccis: siccus, -a, -um,** dry
    natantia: nato, natare, natavi, natatum, swim

19 **turbidum: turbidus, -a, -um,** *adj.,* swollen

20 **infamis: infamis-infame,** *adj.,* ill-famed
    scopulos: scopulus, scopuli, *m.,* cliff, rock
    Acroceraunia: Acroceraunia, Acrocerauniorum, *n. pl.,* a promontory in western
        Greece

21 **nequiquam: nequiquam,** *adv.,* to no avail, in vain
    abscidit: abscindo, abscindere, abscidi, abscissum, cut off from, divide

22 **prudens: prudens, prudentis,** *adj.,* wise, prudent, "in his wisdom"
    dissociabili: dissociabilis-dissociabile, *adj.,* dividing

24 **tangenda: tango, tangere, tetigi, tactum,** touch
    transiliunt: transilio, transilire, transilui, leap over, skim across
    vada: vadum, vadi, *n.,* sea

25 **audax: audax, audacis,** *adj.,* impertinent, bold
    perpeti: perpetior, perpeti, perpessus sum, endure

26 **ruit: ruo, ruere, rui,** rush
    vetitum: veto, vetare, vetavi or **vetui, vetitum,** forbid
    nefas: nefas, *n.,* indeclinable noun meaning something morally wrong

27 **Iapeti: Iapetus, Iapeti,** *m.,* Iapetus; one of the Titans, father of Prometheus,who
        created humankind;
    genus: genus, generis, *n.,* race, family, (figuratively) son

28 **fraude: fraus, fraudis,** *f.,* deceit, theft; *mala* adds the sense of disastrous, asexplained
        in the next lines

29 **aetheria: aetherius, -a, -um,** *adj.,* heavenly
    domo: domus, domus, *f.,* house

maior, tollere seu ponere vult freta.
    quem mortis timuit gradum,
qui siccis oculis monstra natantia,
    qui vidit mare turbidum et
infamis scopulos Acroceraunia?   20
    nequiquam deus abscidit
prudens Oceano dissociabili
    terras, si tamen impiae
non tangenda rates transiliunt vada,
    audax omnia perpeti   25
gens humana ruit per vetitum nefas.
    audax Iapeti genus
ignem fraude mala gentibus intulit.
    post ignem aetheria domo
subductum macies et nova febrium   30
    terris incubuit cohors,
semotique prius tarda necessitas
    leti corripuit gradum.
expertus vacuum Daedalus aera
    pennis non homini datis: 35

30 **macies: macies, maciei,** *f.,* disease
    febrium: febris, febris, *f.,* fever

31 **incubui: incumbo, incumbere, incubui, incubitum,** press upon, bear down on

32 **semotique: semotus, -a, -um,** *adj.,* distant
    prius: prius, *adv.,* previously (to be taken with *semoti* and *tarda)*
    tarda: tardus, -a, -um, *adj.,* slow

32 **necessitas: necessitas, necessitatis,** *f.,* necessity, here inevitability (personified)

33 **leti: letum, leti,** *n.,* death
    corripuit: corripio, corripere, corripui, correptum, hasten, quicken

34 **expertus: experior, experiri, expertus sum,** test, try
    aera: aer, aeris, *m.,* the air

35 **pennis: penna, pennae,** *f.,* wing

perrupit Acheronta Herculeus labor.
    nil mortalibus ardui est:
caelum ipsum petimus stultitia neque
    per nostrum patimur scelus
iracunda Iovem ponere fulmina.   40

36 **perrupit: perrumpo, perrumpere, perrupi, perruptum,** break through; this refers to the attempt by Hercules and Theseus to steal Persephone; the attempt failed; both were confined to Hades, but Hercules was rescued; this theme is also touched upon in *Odes IV.7.*
Acheronta: the river Acheron is here used to denote the lower world in general

37 **ardui: arduus, -a, -um,** *adj.,* difficult, harsh; *ardui* is a genitive of the whole with *nil.* "There is no part too steep or there is nothing too hard." The phrase *nil ardui* has a sense of "too" associated with its use.

38 **stultitia: stultitia, stultitiae,** *f.,* stupidity

39 **scelus: scelus, sceleris,** *n.,* sin, crime

40 **iracunda: iracundus, -a, -um,** *adj.,* angry, wrathful
ponere = deponere: depono, deponere, deposui, depositum, put down, put aside

The portrait above comes from the southern frieze of the Ara Pacis Augustae, a monument built between 13 and 9 B.C. Members of the Augustan family are shown gathered either in connection with the monument's inauguration in 13 B.C. or its completion in 9 B.C. The figure above is situated in the background at the extreme eastern end of the family procession. Some scholars have suggested that the head adorned with laurel is a portrait of Maecenas, the patron of the arts under Augustus and the man to whom *Odes* I.1 has been dedicated.

Odes I.5

1 **gracilis: gracilis-gracile,** *adj.,* slender
   rosa: rosa, rosae, *f.,* rose
   Note the contraposition and chiasmus.

2 **perfusus: perfundo, perfundere, perfudi, perfusum,** steep, drench
   liquidis: liquidus, -a, -um, *adj.,* flowing, clear, liquid
   odoribus: odor, odoris, *m.,* scent, perfume; **urget: urgeo, urgere, ursi,** court

3 **Pyrrha: Pyrrha, Pyrrhae,** *f.,* Pyrrha, a made-up name for the girl who is the
      centerpiece of this poem; the name is Greek, suggesting a girl with brightly
      colored hair.
   antro: antrum, antri, *n.,* grotto, cave

4 **flavam: flavus, -a, -um,** *adj.,* blond; in a country where most people had dark hair,
      blond hair was rare and therefore admired.
   religas: religo, religare, religavi, religatum, tie back; this is a suggestive detail
      implying seduction of the youth by the woman.
   comam: coma, comae, *f.,* hair

5 **simplex: simplex, simplicis,** *adj.,* plain, uncluttered, simple (in regard to adornments
      or other beauty enhancements)
   munditiis: munditia, munditiae, *f.,* cleanliness, elegance; the plural form of this
      abstract noun may suggest the various ways in which Pyrrha demonstrates her
      refined taste without being ostentatious.
   heu: heu, *interj.,* Alas! (Ah! is perhaps the modern equivalent.)
   fidem mutatosque deos = fidem mutatam deorum

6 **mutatosque: muto, mutare, mutavi, mutatum,** change
   flebit: fleo, flere, flevi, fletum, lament, cry over
   aspera: asper-aspera-asperum, *adj.,* rough, roughened

7 **nigris ... ventis:** The clouds of the storm are dark but the epithet has been shifted
      from the clouds to the wind that brings them. The interlocking word order
      enhances the image *(aspera nigris aequora ventis).*

8 **emirabitur: emiror, emirari, emiratus sum,** be amazed at
   insolens: insolens, insolentis, *adj.,* unused, unaccustomed (to such fickleness)

9 **fruitur: fruor, frui, fruitus/fructus sum,** enjoy (with ablative)
   credulus: credulus, -a, -um, *adj.,* believing confidently
   aurea: aureus, -a, -um, *adj.,* golden (modifies *Te* in the ablative case)

10 **vacuum: vacuus, -a, -um,** *adj.,* unattached, detached, available
   amabilem: amabilis-amabile, *adj.,* worthy of love
   Supply *futuram esse* with both *vacuum* and *amabilem.*

handwritten header annotations:
4th Asclepiadean lwlw < SCCI > ASCLEPIADEAN
SCCI
SC — Pherecratean = --|-∪∪-|-
SC ∺ Glyconic = --|-∪∪-|∪

From his experience with the seductive Pyrrha, the poet offers advice to a young man who is "out of his depth" with such a woman. Horace cautions against the woman's temper and the quick and unexpected way that weather changes on the sea of love. Nautical imagery abounds in the poem. The meter is fourth Asclepiadean.

handwritten: contraposition

handwritten: dx ⊃ Quis multa gracilis te puer in rosa *abl plu*

perfusus liquidis urget odoribus *perf pass p*

grato, Pyrrha, sub antro?

cui flavam religas comam,

simplex munditiis? heu quotiens fidem *acc do* 5

mutatosque deos flebit et aspera

nigris aequora ventis

emirabitur insolens, *fut 3sg ind*

qui nunc te fruitur credulus aurea,

qui semper vacuam, semper amabilem 10

sperat, nescius aurae

fallacis! miseri, quibus *dat w/ verb*

intemptata nites. me tabula sacer

votiva paries indicat uvida *d sg pres act ind*

suspendisse potenti *perf act inf dds* 15

vestimenta maris deo. *nom, acc do*

handwritten left margin: it was custom for shipwrecked sailors to hang up clothes ~ metaphor for surviving turbulent relationships

11 **sperat: spero, sperare, speravi, speratum,** hope
nescius: nescius, -a, -um, *adj.,* ignorant of, not knowing (with genitive)
aurae: aura, aurae, *f.,* breeze, wind

12 **fallacis: fallax, fallacis,** *adj.,* deceptive, treacherous

13 **intemptata: intemptatus, -a, -um,** *adj.,* untried
nites: niteo, nitere, nitui, (with dative) dazzle
tabula: tabula, tabulae, *f.,* tablet, picture; frequently sailors who had escaped shipwreck dedicated a votive picture *(tabula)* depicting the catastrophe, together with the clothes they had worn, in the Temple of Neptune.

14 **votiva: votivus, -a, -um,** *adj.,* votive, belonging to a vow, promised by a vow, given in consequence of a vow; **paries: paries, parietis,** *f.,* wall (interior)
indicat: indico, indicare, indicavi, indicatum, show; **uvida: uvidus, -a, -um,** *adj.,* wet

15 **suspendisse: suspendo, suspendere, suspendi, suspensum,** hang up

16 **vestimenta: vestimentum, vestimenti,** *n.,* garment, clothing

Odes I.9

1   **nive: nix, nivis,** *f.,* snow; **ut: ut,** *conj.,* how
   candidum: candeo, candere, candidi, candidum, shine, gleam

2   **Soracte: Soracte, Soractis,** *n.,* Soracte, a mountain near Horace's villa
   sustineant: sustineo, sustinere, sustinui, sustentum, hold up, support, sustain,
      bear
   onus: onus, oneris, *n.,* burden

3   **laborantes** = straining
   geluque: gelu, gelus, *n.,* icy coldness, frost, ice; associated with old age, death

4   **constiterint: consisto, consistere, constiti, constitutum,** come to a stop, come to
      rest, stand still
   acuto: acutus, -a, -um, *adj.,* sharp; bitter

5   **dissolve: dissolvo, dissolvere, dissolvi, dissolutum,** break up, dispel
   frigus: frigus, frigoris, *n.,* the cold; associated with lack of passion or affection
   ligna: lignum, ligni, *n.,* wood, timber
   foco: focus, foci, *m.,* fireplace, hearth

6   **large: large,** *adv.,* copiously, generously; "high"
   reponens: repono, reponere, reposui, repositum, replenish, pile
   benignius: *comp. adv.,* from **benignus, -a, -um,** *adj.,* generous, kindly; here more
      generously (than usual)

7   **deprome: depromo, depromere, deprompsi, depromptum,** bring out, take out
   quadrimum: quadrimus, -a, -um, *adj.,* four-year-old
   Sabina: Sabinus, -a, -um, *adj.,* Sabine, an ancient people of Italy

8   **Thaliarche: Thaliarchus, Thaliarchi,** *m.,* Thaliarchus; this name may deriuve
      from the Greek word θαλια, the muse of comedy, and the verb αρχω, rule; the
      name could mean "master of festivities
   merum: merum, meri, *n.,* wine unmixed with water
   diota: diota, diotae, *f.,* a two-handled wine jug, from the Greek, *dis ous,* "two
      ears"

9   **permitte: permitto, permittere, permisi, permissum,** entrust
   divis: divus, divi, *m.,* god
   simul = simul ac = as soon as

10   **stravere: sterno, sternere, stravi, stratum,** calm, still
   fervido: fervidus, -a, -um, *adj.,* boiling, seething, turbulent

11   **deproeliantis: deproelior, deproeliari, deproeliatus sum,** fight it out, battle fiercely
      (with one another)

handwritten annotations at top:
212 CI {ln¹ / ln²} ‑‑/‑/∪/‑‑ / Alcaic meter
    ‑∪∪‑/∪‑

212 TS l.ne3 ‑/‑∪/‑ ‑‑/‑∪/‑‑

OOTS line4 ‑∪∪/‑∪∪/‑∪/ ‑‑

From the top of the snow-covered slopes of Mount Soracte, a mountain near Horace's villa in the town of Tivoli, the poem moves to the warmth of the hearth inside the house. The frigid inertia of the winter scene outside is countered by the taste of wine and the feel of a warm fire heaped up with freshly cut logs. Such a moment of contrast invites the poet to muse to his young attendant about the past (perhaps his own past), and the preciousness of time, youth and love. The poem anticipates the theme explored more directly in *Odes* I.11, and introduces Alcaic meter, the most common in the *Odes*.

(with handwritten annotations: nom, subject, nom subj, 3 pl pres act subj, abl w/ prep, dative, act pres participle, adv, dat of purpose, Tmesis)

Vides ut alta stet nive candidum
Soracte, nec iam sustineant onus
    silvae laborantes, geluque
        flumina constiterint acuto.
dissolve frigus ligna super foco
large reponens atque benignius
    deprome quadrimum Sabina,
        O Thaliarche, merum diota:
permitte divis cetera, qui simul
stravere ventos aequore fervido   10
    deproeliantis, nec cupressi
        nec veteres agitantur orni
quid sit futurum cras fuge quaerere et
quem Fors dierum cumque dabit lucro
        appone, nec dulcis amores   15

11 **cupressi: cupressus, cupressi,** *f.,* cypress tree, a tall slender tree and hence subject
        to the action of the wind(s)

12 **agitantur: agito, agitare, agitavi, agitatum,** toss
    orni: ornus, orni, *f.,* mountain ash (tree)

13 **cras: cras,** *adv.,* tomorrow; **fuge:** a poetic equivalent of *noli*

14 **Fors: fors, fortis,** *f.,* chance, fate
    lucro: lucrum, lucri, *n.,* gain, profit (dative of purpose)
    quem...cumque: tmesis; **quisquae-quaeque-quidque,** *interog. adj.,* whichever;
        dierum is dependent upon *quemcumque,* "whatever of days" equivalent to "each
        day"

15 **appone: appono, apponere, apposui, appositum,** (with dative) reckon; with *lucro,*
        set down as profit (a technical term in bookkeeping)

Mount Soracte is located near the modern town of Tivoli located about 25 miles east of Rome. This view of one side of Mount Soracte was taken from the ruins of a late republican villa, thought by some to be the villa given to Horace by the emperor Augustus. It is this mountain which the poet refers to in *Odes* I.9, an imposing and impressive sight which could easily have sported snow upon its peak.

Chiasmus

↳ sperne puer neque tu choreas,
donec virenti canities abest
morosa. nunc et campus et areae
   lenesque sub noctem susurri   *nom subj*
      composita repetantur hora,   20
nunc et latentis proditor intimo
gratus puellae risus ab angulo   *subj*
   pignusque dereptum lacertis
      aut digito male pertinaci.

16 **sperne: sperno, spernere, sprevi, spretum,** scorn, reject, pass up
    choreas: chorea, choreae, *f.,* dance

17 **donec: donec,** *conj.,* while, as long as
    virenti: vireo, virere, virui, be fresh, be green, flourish, be full of youthful vigor
        (supply *tibi*)
    canities: canities, canitiei, *f.,* grayness, old age

18 **morosa: morosus, -a, -um,** *adj.,* crabby, grumpy
    campus: campus, campi, *m.,* the Campus Martius
    areae: area, areae, *f.,* an open public space, playground

19 **lenesque: lenis-lene,** *adj.,* soft, gentle; **sub noctem** = at nightfall
    susurri: susurrus, susurri, *m.,* whisper

20 **composita: compono, componere, composui, compositum,** plan, arrange;
        "appointed"
    repetantur: repeto, repetere, repetivi, repetitum, return to, recollect

21 **latentis: lateo, latere, latui,** lie hidden, remain, obscure
    proditor: proditor, proditoris, *m.,* traitor, betrayer (in apposition with *risus*)
    intimo: intimus, -a, -um, *adj.,* innermost, remotest

22 **risus: risus, -us,** *m.,* laughter
    angulo: angulus, anguli, *m.,* nook, corner

23 **pignusque: pignus, pignoris,** *n.,* pledge; ring or bracelet generally worn on the
        upper arm rather than the wrist
    dereptum: deripio, deripere, deripui, dereptum, pull off, snatch away
    lacertis: lacertus, lacerti, *m.,* upper arm

24 **digito: digitus, digiti,** *m.,* finger
    male: male, *adv.,* badly, faintly, barely resisting
    pertinaci: pertinax, pertinacis, *adj.,* tenacious, unyielding, resisting

Odes I.10

1   **Mercuri: Mercurius, Mercuri(i),** *m.,* Mercury, messenger of the gods, god of
    diplomacy, merchants, and wrestling
    facunde: facundus, -a, -um, *adj.,* eloquent
    nepos: nepos, nepotis, *m.,* grandson
    Atlantis: Atlas, Atlantis, *m.,* the giant Atlas; Mercury was the son of Jupiter and
    Atlas' daughter Maia.

2   **feros: ferus, -a, -um,** *adj.,* wild, savage
    cultus: cultus, cultus, *m.,* ways, manners
    recentum: recens, recentis, *adj.,* recent, recently created; primitive

3   **voce: vox, vocis,** *f.,* voice, speech language (by the gift of language)
    formasti: formo, formare, formavi, formatum, form, transform
    catus: catus, -a, -um, *adj.,* clever; here used adverbially with *formasti*
    decorae: decorus, -a, -um, *adj.,* fitting, proper

4   **more: mos, moris,** *m.,* custom, manner, institution
    palaestrae: palaestra, palaestrae, *f.,* a place for wrestling; used here to suggest
    athletic exercise which leads to physical beauty; *decorae* modifies *palaestrae:*
    "with the gift of language and the institution of graceful athletic exercise"

5   **canam: cano, canere, cecini, cantum,** sing
    Iovis: Iuppiter, Jovis, *m.,* Jupiter

6   **nuntium: nuntius, nunti(i),** *m.,* messenger
    curvaeque: curvus, -a, -um, *adj.,* curved
    lyrae: lyra, lyrae, *f.,* lyre
    parentem: parens, parentis, *m.,* author; inventor

7   **callidum: callidus, -a, -um,** *adj.,* clever
    placuit: placeo, placere, placui, placitum, please; "strike one's fancy"
    iocoso: iocosus, -a, -um, *adj.,* playful

8   **condere: condo, condere, condidi, conditum,** hide; take with *callidum*
    furto: furtum, furti, *n.,* trick, theft

9   **boves: bos, bovis,** *f.,* ox
    olim: olim, *adv.,* once; modifies the sentence as a whole and introduces a special
    instance of theft in the next stanza.
    reddidisses: reddo, reddere, reddidi, redditum, return

10 **dolum: dolum, doli,** *n.,* deceit, trick
    amotas: amoveo, amovere, amovi, amotum, steal
    minaci: minax, minacis, *adj.,* threatening

In hymn-like form, this ode offers praise to the god Mercury. Playful references to several events of the god's past life highlight his roles as presider over athletics, messenger god, inventor of the lyre, thief of Apollo's cattle, and concealer of Priam amid the campfires of the Greeks. Lines 9-12 allude to the time when Mercury, as a young boy, was charged by Apollo with stealing his cattle. While Apollo ranted and raved, Mercury tried to steal his quiver. Seeing the humor of it all, Apollo laughed. Mercury, escort of the dead, is pleasing to both the gods above and those below. The meter is Sapphic.

> Mercuri, facunde nepos Atlantis,
> qui feros cultus hominum recentum
> voce formasti catus et decorae
>   more palaestrae,
> te canam, magni Iovis et deorum   5
> nuntium curvaeque lyrae parentem,
> callidum quidquid placuit iocoso
>   condere furto.
> te, boves olim nisi reddidisses
> per dolum amotas, puerum minaci   10
> voce dum terret, viduus pharetra
>   risit Apollo.
> quin et Atridas duce te superbos
> Ilio dives Priamus relicto

11 **terret: terreo, terrere, terrui, territum,** frighten
    viduus: viduus, -a, -um, *adj.,* deprived of (with ablative)
    pharetra: pharetra, pharetrae, *f.,* quiver

12 **risit: rideo, ridere, risi, risum,** laugh
    Apollo: Apollo, Apollinis, *m.,* Apollo, god of the sun, poetry, prophesy

13 **quin et: quin et,** *adv.,* furthermore
    Atridas: Atrides, Atridae, *m.,* Agamemnon and Menelaus (sons of Atreus)
    duce te: ablative absolute
    superbos: superbus, -a, -um, *adj.,* proud, haughty

14 **Ilio: Ilium, Ili(i),** *n.,* Troy
    dives: dives, divitis, *adj.,* rich; perhaps a reference to the ransom which Priam was
        intending to give Achilles (*Iliad* 24.334) in exchange for the body of his beloved
        son Hector
    Priamus: Priamus, Priami, *m.,* Priam, king of Troy
    relicto: relinquo, relinquere, reliqui, relictum, leave

15 **Thessalosque: Thessalus, -a, -um,** *adj.,* Thessalian, the country of northern Greece
from which Achilles and his Myrmidons came
ignis: ignis, ignis, *m.,* fire
iniqua: iniquus, -a, -um, *adj.,* hostile; dative dependent upon *iniqua*

16 **fefellit: fallo, fallere, fefelli, falsum,** pass by unnoticed, slip by; *fefellit* governs
Atridasa ... ignis ... castra.

17 **pias: pius, -a, -um,** *adj.,* pious, loyal
laetis: laetus, -a, -um, *adj.,* happy, blessed
reponis: repono, reponere, reposui, repositum, conduct

18 **virgaque: virga, virgae,** *f.,* the magic wand, *caduceus*
levem: levis-leve, *adj.,* light; ghostly
coerces: coerceo, coercere, coercui, coercitum, keep in order, herd

19 **aurea: aureus, -a, -um,** *adj.,* golden
turbam: turba, tubae, *f.,* throng, crowd
superis: superus, -a, -um, *adj.,* high above; (used substantively) the places of the
gods above

20 **gratus: gratus, -a, -um,** *adj.,* pleasing, welcome
imis: imus, -a, -um, *adj.,* bottom, below; the places of the gods below

Thessalosque ignis et iniqua Troiae   15
     castra fefellit.
tu pias laetis animas reponis
sedibus virgaque levem coerces
aurea turbam, superis deorum
     gratus et imis.   20

This photo shows a circle with astrological quadrants which were carved into the stairs of the Basilica Julia in the Roman Forum. Witnesses waiting to give testimony in court may have frequented astrologers or fortunetellers, who gathered on the steps of the busy court to ply their trade. Perhaps this is the practice which Horace envisions in *Odes* I.11.

Odes I.11

1 **quaesieris: quaero, quaerere, quaesivi, quaesitum,** search for, ask; *quaesieris* and *temptaris* in line 3 are perfect tense subjunctives in a prohibition; the use of the perfect subjunctive with *ne* in place of the present subjunctive is colloquial.

    nefas: nefas, *n.,* an indeclinable word which means something that is morally wrong or impious

2 **Leuconoe: Leuconoe, Leuconoes,** *f.,* Leuconoe, name of a girl; the Greek word λευκος means "clear"; νους "mind". The implication is that Leuconoe is a "clear-thinker".

    Babylonios: Babylonius, -a, -um, *adj.,* Babylonian (Chaldean), a people long famous for astrology

3 **temptaris = temptaveris**

    ut: ut, an exclamatory *adv.,* how, how much better

    numeros: numerus, numeri, *m.,* number; astrology.

    pati: patior, pati, passus sum, experience, suffer, undergo

4 **pluris = plures**

    hiemes: hiems, hiemis, *f.,* winter storm, winter

    tribuit: tribuo, tribuere, tribui, tributum, allot, bestow, give

    ultimam: modifies *hiemem,* the understood object of tribuit and the antecedant of *quae*

5 **oppositis: oppono, opponere, opposui, oppositum,** oppose

    debilitat: debilito, debilitare, debilitavi, debilitatum, exhaust, weaken

    pumicibus: pumex, pumicis, *m.,* soft rock; ablative "against" is understood.

6 **Tyrrhenum: Tyrrhenus, -a, -um,** *adj.,* Etruscan; *mare Tyrrhenum* the Tyrrhenian Sea, from Corsica to Sicily's shore

    sapias: sapio, sapere, sapii, have good taste, be wise (iussive subjunctive)

    liques: liquo, liquare, liquavi, liquatum, strain (iussive subjunctive); this reference alludes to the process of straining pulp from wine; the pulp suggests negative aspects of living, while the strained wine represents good, prudent living.

    spatio: spatium, spati(i), *n.,* span (of life); ablative case expressing cause

7 **reseces: reseco, resecare, resecui, resectum,** prune, cut back (iussive subjunctive)

    invida: invidus, -a, -um, *adj.,* envious, jealous; *aetas* is *invida* because it begrudges us of the enjoyment of life.

Addressed to the otherwise unknown Leuconoe, this poem's modest three sentences convey a densely-packed, cautionary message in the famous words, *carpe diem*. Humankind's anxiety over what tomorrow will or will not bring, expressed in frequent attempts to foretell the future, wastes the precious time of living. The hostile tossing of the seas may have to be endured, but the pleasure of "straining" (*liques* line 6) the wine becomes a metaphor for distilling the real meaning of life. "Cutting back" (*reseces* line 7) suggests pruning of the vine in which one places hope for an abundant harvest. In short, each day of one's life must be plucked. The meter is fifth Asclepiadean.

[handwritten: 2sg perfact subjunc]
[handwritten: subjectve inf]
[handwritten: syncope]

Tu ne quaesieris, scire nefas, quem mihi, quem tibi *[handwritten: datio]*
finem di dederint, Leuconoe, nec Babylonios *[handwritten: voc da]*
temptaris numeros. ut melius, quidquid erit, pati,
seu pluris hiemes seu tribuit Iuppiter ultimam, *[handwritten: de acc adj]*
quae nunc oppositis debilitat pumicibus mare *[handwritten: 5 abl means]*

[handwritten: metaphor →]

Tyrrhenum: sapias, vina liques, et spatio brevi *[handwritten: 2sg presact subjunc]*
spem longam reseces. dum loquimur, fugerit invida *[handwritten: 1pl prespass ind]*
aetas: carpe diem, quam minimum credula postero.
[handwritten: nom subj] *[handwritten: d w/adj]*

[handwritten:]
5th Asclepiadean
S Ç Ç Ç I
$-\,\smile\,|\,-\,\smile\smile\,-\,|\,-\,\smile\smile\,-\,|\,-\,\smile\smile\,-\,|\,\smile\,-$

8   **carpe: carpo, carpere, carpsi, carptum,** pluck, pick, enjoy
quam: quam, *adv.,* (with a superlative degree) as...as possible
credula: credulus, -a, -um, *adj.,* (with dative) trusting, believing in
postero: posterus, -a, -um, *adj.,* next, following, ensuing; (used substantively) the
    future

Odes I.13

1   **Lydia: Lydia, Lydiae,** *f.,* Lydia, the real or fictitious girlfriend of Horace
    Telephi: Telephus, Telephi, *m.,* Telephus, a king of Mysia, son of Heracles and
        Auge, who was once wounded by a spear of Achilles and then cured through
        its rust; probably the reference here uses Telephus as a symbol of the lover who
        has been cured from the disease of love.

2   **cervicem: cervix, cervicis,** *m.,* neck
    roseam: roseus, -a, -um, *adj.,* rosy, rose colored, pink
    cerea: cereus, -a, -um, *adj.,* waxen, of wax; smooth and white as wax

3   **bracchia: bracchium, bracchi(i),** *n.,* arm; **vae: vae,** *interj.,* ah! alas!

4   **fervens: ferveo, fervere,** be boiling hot, boil; burn
    difficili: difficilis-difficile, *adj.,* difficult, harsh, angry
    bile: bilis, bilis, *f.,* bile, anger, wrath
    tumet: tumeo, tumere, tumui, swell; **iecur: iecur, iecuris,** *n.,* the liver

5   **certa sede manent:** *mens* and *clamor* are the subjects of *manent; certa sede,* in a
      sure spot (seat) implies that the speaker is being driven out of his mind; "neither
      my mind nor my complexion remain in a sure state."

6   **umor: umor, umoris,** *m.,* moistness, a liquid, moist tears
    genas: genae, genarum, *f. pl.,* cheeks

7   **furtim: furtim,** *adv.,* secretly; i.e., despite efforts to conceal the tears
    labitur: labor, labi, lapsus sum, slide
    arguens: arguo, arguere, argui, argutum, make known, prove, disclose

8   **quam: quam,** *adv.,* how; taken with lentis; "with what lingering fires"
    lentis: lentus, -a, -um, *adj.,* slow, slow-burning, lingering
    penitus: penitus, *adv.,* from the bottom of the heart, deep down, within
    macerer: macero, macerare, maceravi, maceratum, worry, fret, be mentally
      tortured

9   **Uror: uro, urere, ussi, ustum,** burn, burn up, destroy by fire
    seu: seu or **sive,** *conj.,* or if
    tibi: dative of reference, often used in place of a possessive adjective
    candidos: candidus, -a, -um, *adj.,* shining, white, clear

10   **turparunt = turpaverunt: turpo, turpare, turpavi, turpatum,** disfigure, scar
      (i.e., made black and blue)
    umeros: umerus, umeri, *m.,* shoulder
    immodicae: immodicus, -a, -um, *adj.,* getting out of hand, excessive,
      unrestrained
    mero: merum, meri, *n.,* unmixed wine; this ablative of cause is taken with the
      adjective *immodicae.*

The jealous speaker complains that his girlfriend Lydia talks too much about her new love Telephus. She seems not to realize how much her constant praising of Telephus hurts the speaker, who describes quite graphically the physical effects of passionate love. In the final two stanzas, however, the poet steps back, and in the role of observer offers a more philosophical commentary on the nature of human love. The Lydia of this poem may be an abstraction used by Horace for the purpose of extolling a love that endures, namely a non-passionate one. The meter, like that of *Odes* I.3, is second or lesser Asclepiadean.

[handwritten annotations: "2nd Asclepiadean"; "line 1 Glyconic ScI"; "nom" above "tu"; "—|-ᴜᴜ-|ᴜ_"; "line 2 Ascl ScCI"; "—|-ᴜᴜ-|-ᴜᴜ-|ᴜ_"]

    Cum tu, Lydia, Telephi
cervicem roseam, cerea Telephi *[nom?]*
    laudas bracchia, vae meum
fervens difficili bile tumet iecur. *[dat, abl]*
tum nec mens mihi nec color   5
    certa sede manent, umor et in genas *[dat abl]*
furtim labitur, arguens
    quam lentis penitus macerer ignibus *[adj]* *[non]*
Uror, seu tibi candidos *[1 sg pres passind]*
    turparunt umeros immodicae mero   10
rixae, sive puer furens *[adj]*
    impressit memorem dente labris notam.
non, si me satis audias,
    speres perpetuum dulcia barbare *[adv]*

11 **rixae: rixa, rixae,** *f.,* quarrel, fight
    furens: furens, furentis, *adj.,* raging, wild

12 **impressit: imprimo, imprimere, impressi, impressum,** press upon, imprint, mark
    memorem: memor, memoris, *adj.,* mindful, remembering; as a reminder
    dente: dens, dentis, m., tooth; the poetic singular is used for the plural (ablative of means)
    labris: labrum, labri, *n.,* lip; "on (or upon) your lips"
    notam: nota, notae, *f.,* mark, impression

13 **satis: satis,** *adv.,* enough, "as much as you should"

14 **speres: spero, sperare, speravi, speratum,** hope for, expect; the word takes indirect statement with the words *eum futurum esse* omitted by ellipsis; *perpetuum* is a predicate accusative with *eum*.

laedentem oscula quae Venus   15
quinta <u>parte</u> sui nectaris imbuit. *pop*
 felices ter et amplius
quos irrupta tenet copula nec malis
 divulsus <u>querimoniis</u>   *dat adj*
suprema citius solvet amor die.   20

14 **dulcia: dulcis-dulce**, *adj.,* sweet
 barbare: barbare, *adv.,* barbarously

15 **laedentem: laedo, laedere, laesi, laesum,** hurt
 oscula: osculum, osculi, *n.,* little mouth, kiss; lips.

16 **quinta: quintus, -a, -um,** *adj.,* a fifth; *quinta pars* = quintessence
 sui: suus, -a, -um, *adj.,* her/his/its own; this refers to Venus.
 nectaris: nectar, nectaris, *n.,* the drink of the gods, nectar
 imbuit: imbuo, imbuere, imbui, imbutum, soak, steep

17 **amplius: amplius,** *adv.,* more; *ter et amplius* is a slight variation of the ordinary
  phrase *terque quaterque.*
 Lines 17-20 would read: *felices ter et amplius (sunt ei) quos irrupta copula tenet*
  (et quos) amor malis querimoniis divulsus non solvet citius suprema die.

18 **irrupta = inrupta: inruptus, -a, -um,** *adj.,* unbroken (here with the sense of
  "unbreakable")
 copula: copula, copulae, *f.,* bond; after *nec* understand *quos,* "nor whom"
 nec = et … non

19 **divulsus: divello, divellere, divelli, divulsum,** tear apart, tear to pieces
 querimoniis: querimonia, quaerimoniae, *f.,* difference of opinion, complaint

20 **suprema: supremus, -a, -um,** *adj.,* final, last; *suprema die* = death
 citius: citius, *adv.,* sooner; derived from *citus, -a, -um, adj.,* swift, rapid, quick;
  "quicker or sooner than death," i.e., "before death"
 solvent: solvo, solvere, solvi, solutum, part, separate
 From *nec* to *die:* "and whom no estrangement will part before the day of death"

A sketch of a first century B.C. relief displayed in the Vatican Museum, and found near the town of Palestrina, the location of a very large temple built for the goddess Fortuna. The warship is transporting legionaries; an alligator is clutching the prow of the ship, and there is a large ram attached to the prow. These details are associated with Egypt and call to mind the ships used by Octavian and Agrippa in the battle of Actium in 31 B.C., an event to which *Odes* I.14 may be alluding.

Odes I.14

1 **referent: refero, referre, retuli, relatum,** carry back

2 **fluctus: fluctus, fluctus,** *m.,* wave
   agis: ago, agere, egi, actum, do; *quid agis* is colloquial for "What are you doing?"
   occupa: occupo, occupare, occupavi, occupatum, take, seize, head for (before the storm hits); *occupo* often is found (as here) with the sense of getting to a place before something else does

3 **portum: portus, portus,** *m.,* port; **ut** = how

4 **nudum: nudus, -a, -um,** *adj.,* stripped
   remigio: remigium, remigi(i), *n.,* rowing, (figuratively) oars
   latus: latus, lateris, *n.,* side

5 **malus: malus, mali,** *m.,* mast
   saucius: saucius, -a, -um, *adj.,* injured, battered
   Africo: Africus, Africi, *m.,* southwest wind

6 **antennaeque: antenna, antennae,** *f.,* rigging
   gemant: gemo, gemere, gemui, gemitum, groan
   funibus: funis, funis, *m.,* rope; ropes were tied lengthwise along the hull from stem to stern to strengthen it.

7 **durare: duro, durare, duravi, duratum,** endure, withstand
   carinae: carina, carinae, *f.,* keel of a ship, hull; (The poetic plural is used here.)

8 **imperiosius: imperiosus, -a, -um,** *adj.,* bossy, imperious; overpowering

9 **integra: integer-integra-integrum,** *adj.,* intact
   lintea: linteum, lintei, *n.,* sail

10 **di:** frequently small images of the gods were set up in the sterns of ships for protection; they have been washed away by the hardships of voyage on the sea and with them by implication their protection.
   pressa: premo, premere, pressi, pressum, hard press, overwhelm
   voces: voco, vocare, vocavi, vocatum, call upon (subjunctive in a relative clause of purpose)
   malo: malum, mali, *n.,* trouble

11 **quamvis: quamvis,** *conj.,* although; governs *iactes* (subjunctive) in line 13
   Pontica: Ponticus, -a, -um, *adj.,* of Pontus; a region of the south coast of the Black Sea, mentioned by Catullus in Poem 4
   pinus: pinus, pini, *f.,* pine; *pinus* and *filia* are appositives with the understood subject of *iactes.*

Written in the fourth Asclepiadean meter, like *Odes* I.5, this poem is addressed to a battered ship which is about to venture forth into rough, new waters. The ship, addressed directly like the vessel in *Odes* I.3, may symbolize the state; the storms may symbolize civil wars or recent battles; the port may symbolize peace. The voyage which has imperiled the ship's helmsman, Augustus, may be both real and metaphorical, since Suetonius does mention that a severe storm damaged Octavian's ship upon its return to Italy after the battle of Actium.

O navis, referent in mare te novi
fluctus! O quid agis? fortiter occupa
    portum! nonne vides ut
      nudum remigio latus,
et malus celeri saucius Africo,   5
antennaeque gemant, ac sine funibus
    vix durare carinae
      possint imperiosius
aequor? non tibi sunt integra lintea,
non di quos iterum pressa voces malo.   10
    quamvis Pontica pinus,
      silvae filia nobilis,
iactes et genus et nomen inutile,
nil pictis timidus navita puppibus
    fidit. tu, nisi ventis   15
      debes ludibrium, cave.

13 **iactes: iacto, iactare, iactavi, iactatum,** boast about
    inutile: inutilis-inutile, *adj.,* useless

14 **pictis: pictus, -a, -um,** *adj.,* painted
    timidus: timidus, -a, -um, *adj.,* timid
    navita: navita, navitae, *m.,* sailor

14 **puppibus: puppis, puppis,** *f.,* stern of a vessel

15 **fidit: fido, fidere, fisus sum,** confide in, trust, believe (with dative)

16 **debes: debeo, debere, debui, debitum,** owe; "doomed to be"
    ludibrium: ludibrium, ludubri(i), *n.,* mockery, plaything

nuper sollicitum quae mihi taedium,
nunc desiderium curaque non levis,
   interfusa nitentis
      vites aequora Cycladas.   20

17 **nuper: nuper,** *adv.,* lately
   sollicitum: sollicitus, -a, -um, *adj.,* anxious, sollicitous
   taedium: taedium, taedi(i), *n.,* weariness

18 **desiderium: desiderium, desiderii,** *n.,* object of desire
   non levis: litotes for *gravissima*

19 **interfusa: interfundo, interfundere, interfudi, interfusum,** flow between
   nitentis: nitens, nitentis, *adj.,* shining, glistening

20 **vites: vito, vitare, vitavi, vitatum,** avoid, shun; subjunctive used as a gentle
    imperative; "Please avoid …"
   Cycladas: Cyclades, Cycladum, *f. pl.,* the Cyclades, a group of islands in the south-
    central portion of the Aegean Sea

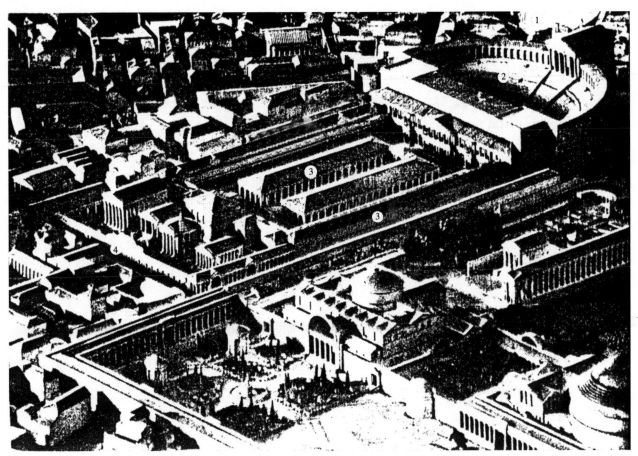

The Opus Pompeianum

1. Temple of Venus Victrix
2. Cavea of the Theater
3. Porticoes
4. Largo Argentina

The Theater of Pompey was dedicated in 55 B.C. and was the first permanent stone theater in Rome. Located in the lower Campus Martius, the theater was close to the Tiber and relatively close to the Vatican hill. Perhaps it is this theater to which Horace refers in *Odes* I.20

Odes I.20

1   **vile: vilis-vile,** *adj.,* cheap
    potabis: poto, potare, potavi, potatum, drink
    modicis: modicus, -a, -um, *adj.,* plain (referring to the material of which they were made)
    Sabinum: Sabinum, Sabini, *n.,* a cheap, local wine, Sabine wine from the Sabine district of Italy

2   **cantharis: cantharus, canthari,** *m.,* a tankard, a drinking vessel with large handles
    Graeca: Graecus, -a, -um, *adj.,* Greek; why does the poet select a Greek jar?
    testa: testa, testae, *f.,* jar

3   **conditum: condo, condere, condidi, conditum,** store up
    levi: lino, linere, levi, litum, smear, daub; seal
    theatro: theatrum, theatri, *n.,* theater

4   **plausus: plausus, plausus,** *m.,* applause; this refers to the return of Maecenas after a long illness; his arrival in the theater was apparently greeted with prolonged applause.

5   **Maecenas: Maecenas, Maecenatis,** *m.,* Maecenas, Horace's friend and patron
    eques: eques, equitis, *m.,* knight
    paterni: paternus, -a, -um, *adj.,* native; the adjective modifies *fluminis* and implies ancestral association of Maecenas and his alleged Etruscan heritage; the Tiber stems from Arezzo, the heart of Etruscan territory in northeastern Italy and the birthplace of Maecenas.

6   **ripae: ripa, ripae,** *f.,* bank of a river
    iocosa: iocosus, -a, -um, *adj.,* merry

7   **redderet: reddo, reddere, reddidi, redditum,** return
    Vaticani: Vaticanus, -a, -um, *adj.,* the Vatican hill, west of the Tiber

8   **imago: imago, imaginis,** *f.,* echo

9   **Caecubum: Caecubum, Caecubi,** *n.,* Caecuban wine, a rather choice wine from the district of Caecubum in southern Latium
    prelo: prelum, preli, *n.,* a wine press
    domitam: domo, domare, domui, domitum, press, crush
    Caleno: Calenus, -a, -um, *adj.,* of Cales, a town in northern Campania famous for fine wine

10 **bibes: bibo, bibere, bibi,** drink; **uvam: uva, uvae,** *f.,* grape; juice of grapes
    Falernae: Falernus, -a, -um, *adj.,* Falernian, a strong, superior wine from the *Falernus ager* in southern Campania

Horace invites his friend Maecenas to drink some homemade wine with him at his villa. The drink, the setting, and the vessels will be simple, but all will be made special by an atmosphere of genuine friendship. Horace has bottled and sealed the wine, set aside specifically for his friend's joyous return. The remote privacy, the simple solace of unsealing and sharing that Sabine wine will stand in contrast to the exaggerated, public and formal recognition otherwise fittingly enjoyed by Maecenas. The contrast of the poet's modest means with the opulence of his invited guest both flatters his patron and echoes a familiar Horatian theme, the virtue of simplicity. The meter is Sapphic as in *Odes* I.10.

> Vile potabis modicis Sabinum
> cantharis, Graeca quod ego ipse testa
> conditum levi, datus in theatro
>   cum tibi plausus,
> care Maecenas eques, ut paterni   5
> fluminis ripae simul et iocosa
> redderet laudes tibi Vaticani
>   montis imago.
> Caecubum et prelo domitam Caleno
> tu bibes uvam: mea nec Falernae   10
> temperant vites neque Formiani
>   pocula colles.

11 **temperant: tempero, temperare, temperavi, temperatum,** flavor, blend
    vites: vitis, vitis, *f.,* vine
    Formiani: Formianus, -a, -um, *adj.,* of Formiae, a coastal town of Latium noted
      for its wine

12 **pocula: poculum, poculi,** *n.,* cup
    colles: collis, collis, *m.,* hill

Odes I.21

1   **dicite = cantate**; **virgines** = maidens

2   **intonsum: intonsus, -a, -um,** *adj.,* with uncut hair, i.e., flowing
       Cynthium: Cynthius, -a, -um, *adj.,* Cynthian; Mt. Cynthos in Delos, the birthplace
          of Apollo

3   **Latonamque: Latona, Latonae,** *f.,* Latona; the mother of Apollo and Diana

4   **dilectam: dilectus, -a, -um,** *adj.,* beloved; **penitus: penitus,** *adv.,* deeply, dearly
       Iovi: Iuppiter, Iovis, *m.,* Jupiter (dative of agent with *dilectam*)

5   **vos = virgines;** supply *dicite Dianam*
       laetam: laetus, -a, -um, *adj.,* happy, (with ablative of specification) delighting in
       fluviis: fluvius, fluvi(i), *m.,* stream, river (ablative with *laetam*)
       nemorum: nemus, nemoris, *n.,* grove
       coma = foliage (ablative with *laetam*)

6   **quaecumque:** indefinite relative pronoun refering to *Dianam* understood in line 5
          and modified by *laetam*
       gelido: gelidus, -a, -um, *adj.,* chilly, cold
       prominet: promineo, prominere, prominui, stand out
       Algido, Algidus, Algidi, *m.,* Mt. Algidus, a mountain southeast of Rome between
          Tusculum and Velitrae, known today as Monte Compatri, long associated with
          the worship of Diana

7   **nigris: niger, nigra, nigrum,** *adj.,* dark, gloomy; the dark green of the oaks and
          birches of Erymanthus is contrasted with the light green of Cragus.
       Erymanthi: Erymanthus, Erymanthi, *m.,* Mt. Erymanthus in northern Arcadia,
          a section of the northwestern Peloponnesus

8   **Cragi: Cragus, Cragi,** *m.,* Mt. Cragus, a mountain in Lycia in Asia Minor, the
          home of Leto (Latona)

9   **Tempe: Tempe,** *n.,* (indeclinable) Tempe, a valley in northern Greece between
          Thessaly and Macedonia, associated with the worship of Apollo
       totidem: totidem, indeclinable *adj.* just as many, i.e., just as many as Diana
       tollite: tollo, tollere, sustuli, sublatum, extol
       laudibus: laus, laudis, *f.,* praise

10   **natalemque: natalis-natale,** *adj.,* natal, (as a substantive) birthplace
       mares: mas, maris, *m.,* male; *mares = pueri*
       Delon: Delos, Deli, *f.,* the island of Delos

11   **insignem: insignis-insigne,** *adj.,* distinguished; this word modifies *Apollinem*
          (understood); *umerum* in line 12 is an accusative of respect after *insignem.*
       pharetra: pharetra, pharetrae, *f.,* quiver

This hymn praises Diana and Apollo. The occasion has been thought by some to be the dedication of the Temple of Apollo on the Palatine Hill in 28 B.C., but the tone of this poem seems too casual for such a formal occasion. The poem compares well with Catullus 34. The meter is fourth Asclepiadean, seen earlier in *Odes* I.5.

> Dianam tenerae dicite virgines,
> intonsum, pueri, dicite Cynthium
>   Latonamque supremo
>   dilectam penitus Iovi.
> vos laetam fluviis et nemorum coma,   5
> quaecumque aut gelido prominet Algido
>   nigris aut Erymanthi
>   silvis aut viridis Cragi.
> vos Tempe totidem tollite laudibus
> natalemque, mares, Delon Apollinis,   10
>   insignemque pharetra
>   fraternaque umerum lyra.
> hic bellum lacrimosum, hic miseram famem
> pestemque a populo et principe Caesare in
>   Persas atque Britannos   15
>   vestra motus aget prece.

12 **fraterna: fraternus, -a, -um,** *adj.,* brother's; this modifies *lyra* and depends in sense upon the adjective *insignem* ; *pharetra* and *lyra* are both ablative case expressing cause;
umerus, umeri, *m.,* shoulder
Mercury (Hermes) is the brother of Apollo, since they were both sons of Jupiter; Mercury had invented the lyre but gave it to Apollo intending to atone partially for the earlier stealing his cattle.

13 **hic** refers to Apollo.; **lacrimosum: lacrimosus, -a, -um,** *adj.,* tearful
famem: fames, famis, *f.,* hunger

14 **pestemque: pestis, pestis,** *f.,* disease, plague
principe: princeps, principis, *m.,* leader; **in** = against

15 **Persas: Persae, Persarum,** *m. pl.,* the Persians (Parthians), people of the Far East
Brittannos: Brittanni, Brittannorum, *m. pl.,* the Britons, people of the Far West

16 **motus: moveo, movere, movi, motum,** move, touch (modifies *hic*)
aget: ago, agere, egi, actum, drive away
prece: prex, precis, *f.,* prayer; this word is more commonly found in the plural.

Odes I.22

1 **integer: integer-integra-integrum,** *adj.,* wholesome, blameless, possessing moral integrity (like *purus* used substantively)
   sceleris: scelus, sceleris, *n.,* crime (the genitives *vitae* and *sceleris* indicate respect; "wholesome in respect to life and blameless in respect to crime")
   purus: purus, -a, -um, *adj.,* clean, wholesome, pure

2 **eget: egeo, egere, egui,** need (with ablative)
   Mauris: Maurus, -a, -um, *adj.,* Moorish, of or pertaining to ferocious warriors in North Africa
   iaculis: iaculum, iaculi, *n.,* javelin
   arcu: arcus, arcus, *m.,* bow

3 **venenatis: venenatus, -a, -um,** *adj.,* poisoned
   gravida: gravidus, -a, -um, *adj.,* heavy

4 **Fusce: Fuscus, Fusci,** *m.,* Aristius Fuscus, a close friend of Horace who wrote comedies and may have been a schoolmaster

5 **Syrtis: Syrtis, Syrtis,** *f.,* shifting sands of North Africa's coast
   iter: iter, itineris, *n.,* journey, (with the verb *facio)* travel
   aestuosas: aestuosus, -a, -um, *adj.,* hot, sweltering

6 **inhospitalem: inhospitalis-inhospitale,** *adj.,* inhospitable, unfriendly

7 **Caucasum: Caucasus, Caucasi,** *m.,* the Caucasus mountains between the Black and Caspian Seas, where Prometheus was chained
   vel quae loca = vel (per ea) loca quae
   fabulosus: fabulosus, -a, -um, *adj.,* fabled; in the sense of "romantic" due to the associations of the Hydaspes river

8 **lambit: lambo, lambere, lambi,** lick, wash, water
   Hydaspes: Hydaspes, Hydaspis, *m.,* Hydaspes river, tributary of the Indus river and associated with Alexander the Great's victory in 326 B.C. over the elephants of Poros; also on this river, Alexander founded Beucephala, a city named after his horse, Beucephalus

9 **namque: namque,** *conj.,* for
   lupus: lupus, lupi, *m.,* wolf

10 **canto: canto, cantare, cantavi, cantatum,** sing; *dum* meaning "while" takes the historical present as here *dum canto* (while I was singing).
   Lalage: Lalage, Lalages, *f.,* Lalage, a made-up name for a girl derived from the Greek verb meaning talking, prattling; "a chatterbox"
   ultra: ultra, *prep.* (with accusative), beyond

Horace wanders past the boundary markers of his property and encounters a fierce wolf. The savage animal flees from him even though he is unarmed, because, as Horace humorously suggests, a lover is so pure of heart that he is free from common dangers. The seeming seriousness of the first two stanzas is immediately undercut by the hyperbole which the poet uses to introduce the wolf and the unarmed wanderer singing of his beloved. In the final two stanzas, the poet's exaggerated claims of eternal devotion gently mock the sentimental romanticism occasionally found in the poetry of his contemporaries. The meter is Sapphic as seen in *Odes* I.10.

> Integer vitae scelerisque purus *gen*
> non eget Mauris iaculis neque arcu *abl*
> nec venenatis gravida sagittis,
>   Fusce, pharetra, *abl, nom*
> sive per Syrtis iter aestuosas   5
> sive facturus per inhospitalem
> Caucasum vel quae loca fabulosus
>   lambit Hydaspes. *3rd sg pres act ind*
> namque me silva lupus in Sabina,
> dum meam canto Lalagen et ultra   10
> terminum curis vagor expeditis,
>   fugit inermem,
> quale portentum neque militaris
> Daunias latis alit aesculetis

11 **terminum: terminus, termini,** *m.,* boundary, limit of property
   vagor: vagor, vagari, vagatus sum, wander
   expeditis: expedio, expedire, expedivi, expeditum, set aside (modifies *curis* in an ablative absolute)

12 **inermem: inermis-inerme,** *adj.,* unarmed

13 **quale: qualis-quale,** *adj.,* of such a sort or kind
   portentum: portentum, portenti, *n.,* monster; in apposition with *lupus,* "such a monster as …"
   militaris: militaris-militare, *adj.,* warlike, bellicose

14 **Daunias: Daunias, Dauniadis,** *f.,* the province of Daunia (Apulia), where Horace's birthplace Venusia was located; there was a tradition that very tough soldiers came from Apulia.
   latis: latus, -a, -um, *adj.,* wide
   alit: alo, alere, alui, alitum, nurture
   aesculetis: aesculetum, aesculeti, *n.,* oak forest

15 **Iubae: Iuba, Iubae,** *m.,* Juba, king of Numidia in Africa
tellus: tellus, telluris, *f.,* land
generat: genero, generare, generavi, generatum, beget, produce
leonum: leo, leonis, *m.,* lion

16 **arida: aridus, -a, -um,** *adj.,* dry, parched
nutrix: nutrix, nutricis, *f.,* nurse; this combination of *arida* and *nutrix* is an oxymoron, an apparent contradiction in terms.

17 The word order of this line is: *pone me (in) pigris campis ubi ...*
pigris: piger-pigra-pigrum, *adj.,* lifeless, barren

18 **aestiva: aestivus, -a, -um,** *adj.,* summer
recreatur: recreo, recreare, recreavi, recreatum, refresh, revive
aura: aura, aurae, breeze

19 **quod latus mundi,** *i.e., in eo latere mundi quod*
latus: latus, lateris, *n.,* side, section; **mundi: mundus, mundi,** *m.,* world
nebulae: nebula, nebulae, *f.,* mist, fog

20 **Juppiter,** metonymy for weather; with *malus,* bad weather
urget: urgeo, urgere, ursi, lower, brood

21 **curru: currus, currus,** *m.,* chariot
nimium: nimium, *adv.,* excessively, too much
propinqui: propinquus, -a, -um, *adj.,* near

22 **solis: sol, solis,** *m.,* sun
domibus: domus, domus, *f.,* home, house
negata: nego, negare, negavi, negatum, deny; *domibus negata* denied to homes, i.e., uninhabitable

23 **dulce: dulce,** *adv.,* derived from *dulcis-dulce, adj.,* sweet
ridentem: rideo, ridere, risi, risum, smile, laugh; this phrase recalls Catullus Poem 51.

24 **loquentem: loquor, loqui, locutus sum,** speak, talk; the participle portrays the meaning of the name Lalage, and this feature, combined with the repetition of *dulce,* outdoes Catullus 51.

nec Iubae tellus generat, leonum   15
    arida nutrix.   *nom*
oxymoron →
pone me pigris ubi nulla campis *dat abl*
arbor aestiva recreatur aura,
quod latus mundi nebulae malusque
    Iuppiter urget;   20
pone sub curru nimium propinqui *2nd sg pres act imp*
solis in terra domibus negata:
dulce ridentem Lalagen amabo,
    dulce loquentem. *pap*

Horace's mention of his encounter with a wolf (*Odes* I.22) brings to mind the famous encounter of Romulus and Remus with the she-wolf. Here is a bronze statue depicting the nurturing of the city founders, Romulus and Remus, by a wolf. This statue, thought to have come from an Etruscan tomb, may be seen in the Capitoline museum in Rome. The infant figures, not part of the original statue, were added in the Renaissance.

Odes I.23

1   **vitas: vito, vitare, vitavi, vitatum,** avoid, shun
    inuleo: (h)in(n)uleus, (h)in(n)ulei, *m.,* fawn
    similis: similis-simile, *adj.,* (with dative) similar to, like (modifies the implied
        subject of the verb *vitas*)
    Chloe: Chloe, Chloes, *f.,* Chloe, a girl's name; from a Greek word which means a
        "green" plant or shoot

2   **quaerenti: quaero, quaerere, quaesivi, quaesitum,** look for, seek
    pavidam: pavidus, -a, -um, *adj.,* panicky, fearful
    aviis: avius, -a, -um, *adj.,* pathless, trackless

3   **vano: vanus, -a, -um,** *adj.,* groundless, empty

4   **aurarum: aura, aurae,** *f.,* breeze
    metu: metus, metus, *m.,* fear

5   **seu: seu … seu,** whether … or
    mobilibus: mobilis-mobile, *adj.,* mobile, quivering
    veris: ver, veris, *n.,* spring
    inhorruit: inhorresco, inhorrescere, inhorrui, rustle

6   **adventus: adventus, adventus,** *m.,* arrival
    foliis: folium, foli(i), *n.,* leaf; (with *in* understood) among the trembling leaves
    virides: viridis-viride, *adj.,* green
    rubum: rubus, rubi, *m.,* bramble

7   **dimovere: dimoveo, dimovere, dimovi, dimotum,** move aside
    lacertae: lacerta, lacertae, *f.,* lizard

8   **corde: cor, cordis,** *n.,* heart
    genibus: genu, genus, *n.,* knee
    tremit: tremo, tremere, tremui, tremble, shake, quiver; subject is *inuleus.*

9   **atqui: atqui,** *conj.,* (a very strong objection) but
    tigris: tigris, tigris, *f.,* tiger; **ut** = like, as
    aspera: asper-aspera-asperum, fierce, rough

10 **Gaetulusve: Gaetulus, -a, -um,** *adj.,* Gaetulian, pertaining to the people of north-
        west Africa
    frangere: frango, frangere, fregi, fractum, crush, maul; note the unusual use of
        the infinitive to serve as a purpose clause.
    persequor: persequor, persequi, persecutus sum, persistently pursue

The poet pretends that he is seriously addressing a young girl who is resisting his advances. Like a nervous fawn, the girl Chloe seeks the protection and security of her mother, whereas the speaker feels that she is ready for a man. This poem is playful, although the references to the conditions that spark the fawn to run to its mother may be symbolic representations of all the dangers that love creates for lovers. The meter is fourth Asclepiadean, seen in *Odes* I.5

> Vitas inuleo me similis, Chloe,
> quaerenti pavidam montibus aviis
>   matrem non sine vano
>   aurarum et silvae metu.
> nam seu mobilibus veris inhorruit   5
> adventus foliis seu virides rubum
>   dimovere lacertae,
>   et corde et genibus tremit.
> atqui non ego te tigris ut aspera
> Gaetulusve leo frangere persequor: 10
>   tandem desine matrem
>   tempestiva sequi viro.

11 **tandem: tandem,** *adv.,* finally, once and for all; *tandem* expresses a strong sense
        of impatience and is best translated: "Now stop following"
    desine: desino, desinere, desii, desitum, cease

12 **tempestiva: tempestivus, -a, -um,** *adj.,* timely, seasonable, age for

Odes I.24

1 **quis:** an interrogative adjective modifying *pudor* and *modus*
desiderio: desiderium, desideri(i), *n.,* longing, desire, grief
sit: deliberative subjunctive
pudor: pudor, pudoris, *m.,* sense of propriety, restraint
modus: modus, modi, *m.,* limit

2 **capitis: caput, capitis,** *n.,* head (metonymy for life)
praecipe: praecipio, praecipere, praecepi, praeceptum, teach (*me* understood)
lugubris: lugubris-lugubre, *adj.,* of mourning

3 **cantus: cantus, cantus,** *m.,* song
Melpomene: Melpomene, Melpomenes, *f.,* Melpomene, the muse of tragedy
liquidam: liquidus, -a, -um, *adj.,* flowing; clear
pater = Jupiter

4 **cithara: cithara, citharae,** *f.,* the lyre

5 **ergo: ergo,** *adv.,* and so, then
Quintilium: Quintilius, Quintili(i), *m.,* Quintilius Varus, a friend of Vergil and of
     Horace, who died in 24 B.C.
sopor: sopor, soporis, *m.,* a deep sleep of death

6 **urget: urgeo, urgere, ursi,** lie heavy on, weigh down
Pudor: Pudor, Pudoris, *m.,* modesty

7 **incorrupta: incorruptus, -a, -um,** *adj.,* unspoiled, genuine
Veritas: veritas, veritatis, *f.,* truth

8 **parem: par, paris,** *adj.,* equal; modifies *ullum*
inveniet: the Latin verb tends to agree with the number of its nearest subject, despite
     the fact that the subject here is compound.

9 **flebilis: flebilis-flebile,** *adj.,* (with dative) causing tears to, mourned by
occidit: occido, occidere, occidi, occasum, die

11 **pius: pius, -a, -um,** *adj.,* devoted (to him)

12 **poscis: posco, poscere, poscui, poscitum,** ask, ask back; the verb takes two
     accusatives, one of the person being asked *(deos)* and one of the thing or person
     being asked for *(Quintilium).*

13 **quid:** supply *prodest* or *prodesset*
Threicio: Threicius, -a, -um, *adj.,* Thracian
blandius: *comp. adv.* from *blandus, -a, -um, adj.,* charming
Orpheo: Orpheus, Orphei, *m.,* the poet Orpheus who attracted the beasts of nature,
     even the trees, to come to listen to his music

Horace extends sympathy to the poet Vergil upon the death of their mutual friend Quintilius. Quintilius is praised explicitly for his qualities of modesty, loyalty, and candor as a literary critic. Vergil's profound grief recalls the story of Orpheus, whose songs, composed to please Hades, were unsuccessful in bringing his wife Eurydice back to life. This poignant myth is used by Horace to help Vergil accept the unalterable fact of Quintilius' death. The meter is third Asclepiadean.

> Quis desiderio sit pudor aut modus
> tam cari capitis? praecipe lugubris
> cantus, Melpomene, cui liquidam pater
>   vocem cum cithara dedit.
> ergo Quintilium perpetuus sopor   5
> urget! cui Pudor et Iustitiae soror,
> incorrupta Fides, nudaque Veritas
>   quando ullum inveniet parem?
> multis ille bonis flebilis occidit,
> nulli flebilior quam tibi, Vergili,   10
> tu frustra pius heu non ita creditum
>   poscis Quintilium deos.
> quid si Threicio blandius Orpheo
> auditam moderere arboribus fidem,
> num vanae redeat sanguis imagini,   15
>   quam virga semel horrida,
> non lenis precibus fata recludere,

14 **moderere = modereris: moderor, moderari, moderatus sum,** play, sound
    arboribus: dative of agency with the perfect passive participle *auditam*
    fidem: fides, fidis, *f.,* chord, lyre

15 **vanae: vanus, -a, -um,** *adj.,* unsubstantial, shadowy
    imagini: imago, imaginis, *f.,* shade, ghost; suggests death masks used in Roman
        funeral processions

16 **virga: virga, virgae,** *f.,* the wand used by Mercury; *virga* is ablative case.
    semel: semel, *adv.,* once

17 **lenis: lenis-lene,** *adj.,* gentle, moderately disposed, "kind to the idea of"; this word
        modifies Mercurius in line 18.
    precibus: prex, pregis, *f.,* prayer; *precibus* is dative indirect object of *lenis.*

nigro compulerit Mercurius gregi?
durum: sed levius fit patientia
    quidquid corrigere est nefas.   20

17 **recludere: recludo, recludere, reclusi, reclusum,** (opposite of *claudere,* close)
    reveal, open, disclose; *fata* is the object of *recludere,* an infinitive with *precibus*;
    fata = *portas fatorum*

18 **nigro: niger, nigra, nigrum,** *adj.,* black, dark, lifeless; the word describes the
    shadowy nature of the souls of the dead.
    compulerit: compello, compellere, compuli, compulsum, herd together, gather,
    collect
    gregi: grex, gregis, *m.,* flock

19 **durum: durus, -a, -um,** *adj.,* hard, difficult; supply *est,* "It is hard to bear."
    levius: a comparative neuter predicate *adj.* from *levis-leve, adj.,* light (in weight);
    but here there is the sense of "easier".
    patientia: patientia, patientiae, *f.,* endurance, patience, resignation; *patientia* is
    ablative case.

20 **corrigere: corrigo, corrigere, correxi, correctum,** set straight, bring into order;
    the infinitive follows *nefas; quidquid* is the subject of *est*; the entire clause
    introduced by *quidquid* serves as the subject of *fit.*
    nefas: (an indeclinable adjective) something unlawful, something forbidden by the
    gods; this word is the opposite of *fas.*

This sketch shows open shutters of the type referred to in *Odes* I.25. The room to which they are attached belongs to an apartment within a large apartment house *(insula)* similar to that perhaps inhabited by Lydia.

Odes I.25

1   **parcius:** *comp. adv.,* from *parcus, -a, -um, adj.,* sparing; less often
    iunctas: iunctus, -a, -um, *adj.,* closed, latched
    quatiunt: quatio, quatere, (no perfect active), **quassum,** shake, beat, strike
    fenestras: fenestra, fenestrae, *f.,* window, shutter

2   **iactibus: iactus, iactus,** *m.,* throwing, casting, toss; the reference is to the throwing
    of stones at the closed shutters on the house of a woman well known for her
    attractiveness.
    crebris: creber-crebra-crebrum, *adj.,* frequent, repeated
    protervi: protervus, -a, -um, *adj.,* shameless, rowdy

3   **adimunt: adimo, adimere, ademi, ademptum,** take away from, deprive
    tibi: a dative of separation with *adimunt*
    somnos: somnus, somni, *m.,* sleep; the poetic plural is used.

4   **limen: limen, liminis,** *n.,* threshold; the door is personified and its love for its
    threshold is best expressed: "the door hugs its threshold."

5   **quae:** refers to *ianua* in line 4, which is personified
    prius: prius, *adv.,* earlier, in the past
    multum: multum., *adv.,* much, very; Horace often uses *multum* with an adverbial
    sense to modify adjectives; "right easily," "right readily"
    facilis: facilis-facile, *adj.,* easy, ready, easily impelled (to take a particular course
    of action), prone

6   **cardines: cardo, cardinis,** *m.,* hinge, pivot

7   **pereunte: pereo, perire, perii or perivi, periturus,** die (a common term used of
    a love-sick person); the ablative of the present participle modifies *me* forming
    an ablative absolute; *tuo* modifies the understood noun *amatore* (lover) and is
    in apposition with *me.* These words suggest that Horace is imitating a particular
    type of love song *(paraclausithyron)* where the "locked out" lover is prostrating
    himself to regain the affection of his lover (see Catullus 8).

8   **dormis: dormio, dormire, dormivi, dormitum,** sleep

9   **invicem: invicem,** *adv.,* in turn; note the emphatic position.
    moechos: moechus, moechi, *m.,* adulterer
    anus: anus, anus, *f.,* an old woman, old maid; in apposition with the subject of
    flebis
    arrogantis = arrogantes: arrogans, arrogantis, *adj.,* insolent, arrogant; they are
    "stuck-up" because they snub Lydia.

Addressed to Lydia, this poem portrays the poet's former lover as old, abandoned, passed over by the young. The first three stanzas present a harshly realistic portrayal of Lydia's growing distance from love's fulfillment. The second three, following a traditional motif of Hellenistic poetry, carry a warning of further frustration in her mad pursuit of lovers. The way cut flowers are discarded as they age, so will she be discarded with a chill, wintery indifference. The meter is Sapphic.

> Parcius iunctas quatiunt fenestras
> iactibus crebris iuvenes protervi,
> nec tibi somnos adimunt amatque
>   ianua limen,
> quae prius multum facilis movebat   5
> cardines; audis minus et minus iam
> 'me tuo longas pereunte noctes,
>   Lydia, dormis?'
> invicem moechos anus arrogantis
> flebis in solo levis angiportu,   10
> Thracio bacchante magis sub inter-
>   lunia vento,
> cum tibi flagrans amor et libido,

10 **flebis: fleo, flere, flevi, fletum,** cry over, shed tears over, lament
    levis: levis-leve, *adj.,* forlorn, worthless; she is worthless because she is unaccompanied by the lover whose presence made her a person of some worth.
    solo: solus, -a, -um, *adj.,* deserted
    angiportu: angiportus, angiportus, *m.,* alley

11 **Thracio: Thracius, -a, -um,** *adj.,* Thracian, from Thrace; modifies *vento*
    bacchante: bacchor, bacchari, bacchatus sum, revel, howl
    magis: magis., *adv.,* more (than usual)
    sub: sub, *prep.,* (with accussative), during, in the course of; just before, at the approach of

12 **interlunia: interlunium, interluni(i),** *n.,* new moon; the plural form suggests "each new moon" or "as each new moon approaches."

13 **tibi:** dative of reference
    flagrans: flagrans, flagrantis, *adj.,* flaming, burning
    libido: libido, libidinis, *f.,* passion, pleasure, lust, sensuality

14 **matres equorum** = *mares*
    furiare: furio, furiare, (no perfect form), **furiatum,** drive mad, madden,
        infuriate

15 **saeviet: saevio, saevire, saevii, saevitum,** rage, rave
    circa: circa, *adv.,* round about, around, near
    iecur: iecur, iecuris, *n.,* liver (the alleged seat of passion); (with *ulcerosus*) wounded
        heart
    ulcerosum: ulcerosus, -a, -um, *adj.,* full of sores, ulcerous

16 **questu: questus, questus,** *m.,* complaint

17 **laeta: laetus, -a, -um,** *adj.,* happy
    pubes: pubes, pubis, *f.,* youth
    hedera: hedera, hederae, *f.,* ivy; modified by *virenti*
    virenti: virens, virentis, *adj.,* fresh, vigorous, flourishing

18 **gaudeat: gaudeo, gaudere, gavisus sum,** be glad, be pleased, rejoice
    pulla: pullus, -a, -um, *adj.,* dark (green), seasoned; modifies *myrto*
    magis atque = rather than; note the contrast between the freshness of ivy and the
        darkness of myrtle, symbolizing the young versus the old.
    myrto: myrtus, myrti, *f.,* myrtle; note that *sed* is understood after *myrto*.

19 **aridas: aridus, -a, -um,** *adj.,* dry
    frondes: frons, frondis, *m., f.,* leaf, foliage
    hiemis: hiems, hiemis, *f.,* winter
    sodali: sodalis, sodalis, *m.,* companion; *hiemis sodali* is in apposition with
        Hebro

20 **dedicet: dedico, dedicare, dedicavi, dedicatum,** dedicate; the implication is that
        a sacrifice will be made, an animal consigned to the gods.
    Hebro: Hebrus, Hebri, *m.,* the Hebrus river in Thrace; the reference to this remote
        northern river creates a recognizable context for the withered ivy and myrtle,
        which must be tossed away now that their season has passed. Horace's metaphor
        from nature makes vivid for the reader the way older women are passed over
        for the younger.

quae solet matres furiare equorum,
saeviet circa iecur ulcerosum,   15
   non sine questu
laeta quod pubes hedera virenti
gaudeat pulla magis atque myrto,
aridas frondes hiemis sodali
   dedicet Hebro.   20

Odes I.34

1 **parcus: parcus, -a, -um,** *adj.,* sparing, stingy
   cultor: cultor, cultoris, *m.,* worshipper
   infrequens: infrequens, infrequentis, *adj.,* infrequent

2 **insanientis: insaniens, insanientis,** *adj.,* insane, mad
   dum: dum, *conj.,* while (with historical present); "while I was wandering."
   sapientiae: sapientia, sapientiae, *f.,* philosophy

3 **consultus: consultus, -a, -um,** *adj.,* (with genitive) adept in, expert in
   erro: erro, errare, erravi, erratum, wander, stray (from the truth)
   retrorsum: retrorsum, *adv.,* backwards

4 **iterare: itero, iterare, iteravi, iteratum,** do (a thing) a second time, repeat
   cursus: cursus, cursus, *m.,* course

5 **cogor: cogo, cogere, coegi, coactum,** force, compel
   relictos: relinquo, relinquere, reliqui, relictum, leave, abandon
   namque: namque, *conj.,* for
   Diespiter: Diespiter, Diespitris, *m.,* old name for Jupiter, god of the sky

6 **corusco: coruscus, -a, -um,** *adj.,* flashing
   nubila: nubilus, -a, -um, *adj.,* cloudy (used substantively)

7 **plerumque: plerumque,** *adv.,* generally, usually
   tonantis: tono, tonare, tonui, tonitum, thunder

8 **volucremque: volucer-volucris-volucre,** *adj.,* swift
   currum: currus, currus, *m.,* chariot

9 **quo:** the antecedent of this relative is the combination of the actions described by
      lines 5-8, namely the flash of lightning as well as the following loud thunder.
   bruta: brutus, -a, -um, *adj.,* inert, dull
   vaga: vagus, -a, -um, *adj.,* wandering

10 **Styx: Styx, Stygis,** *f.,* the Styx, a river of the underworld
   invisi: invisus, -a, -um, *adj.,* hated
   horrida: horridus, -a, -um, *adj.,* awful
   Taenari: Taenarus, Taenari, *m.,* Cape Taenarus, a promontory on the southernmost
      point of the Peloponnesus, associated with an entrance into the underworld
      because the huge cave runs deep into the earth and its floor is covered by a dark
      pool of water.

11 **Atlanteusque: Atlanteus, -a, -um,** *adj.,* related to Atlas, the end of the then known
   world, the extreme west

Horace has heard a clap of thunder in a cloudless sky, prompting him to a mock-serious renunciation of his former scepticism. By the end of the poem, however, this alarming portent reminds him of the power of what he is unable to see, and prompts reflections on the paths of religious practice and belief, which he has not taken seriously enough till now. The mutability of life's fortunes is brought to the fore of his imagination as he reflects on the powers beyond his control, which can turn things upside down and remove anyone's good luck, replacing it with bad. His thinking may indicate a rejection of Epicurean beliefs in favor of Stoic ideals and practices. The meter is Alcaic, like that of *Odes* I.9.

> Parcus deorum cultor et infrequens
> insanientis dum sapientiae
>   consultus erro, nunc retrorsum
>   vela dare atque iterare cursus
> cogor relictos: namque Diespiter,   5
> igni corusco nubila dividens
>   plerumque, per purum tonantis
>   egit equos volucremque currum,
> quo bruta tellus et vaga flumina,
> quo Styx et invisi horrida Taenari   10
>   sedes Atlanteusque finis
>   concutitur. valet ima summis
> mutare et insignem attenuat deus,
> obscura promens; hinc apicem rapax

12 **concutitur: concutio, concutere, concussi, concussum,** shake
   valet: valeo, valere, valui, have power to
   ima: imus, -a, -um, *adj.,* lowest (used substantively)
   summis: summus, -a, -um, *adj.,* top, highest (used substantively)

13 **mutare = commutare** = exchange
   insignem: insignis-insigne, *adj.,* renowned (used substantively)
   attenuat: attenuo, attenuare, attenuavi, attenuatum, humble

14 **obscura: obscurus, -a, -um,** *adj.,* lowly
   promens: promo, promere, prompsi, promptum, bring before the world, exalt
   hinc ... hic (line 16) = "from one person ... to another"
   apicem: apex, apicis, *m.,* tiara, crown
   rapax: rapax-rapacis, *adj.,* rapacious; (with adverbial force) "swiftly"

fortuna cum stridore acuto   15
sustulit, hic posuisse gaudet.

15 **stridore: stridor, -oris,** *m.,* noise, whirring (of wings)
    acuto: acutus, -a, -um, *adj.,* shrill

16 **sustulit: tollo, tollere, sustuli, sublatum,** take away
    posuisse: pono, ponere, posui, positum, place down
    gaudet: gaudeo, gaudere, gavisus sum, delight in, rejoice in

Odes I.37

Horace expresses joy at the defeat and passing of Cleopatra. The ode celebrates both the news of Octavian's victory at Actium in 31 B.C. and his triumph in 29 B.C. The early stanzas refer to Cleopatra as a hated enemy plotting destruction for all that is Roman. The poem turns with the simile in lines 17-20. The balance of the poem seems to elicit respect for Cleopatra's courage in the act of suicide. The meter is Alcaic like *Odes* I.9.

Nunc est bibendum, nunc pede libero
pulsanda tellus, nunc Saliaribus
   ornare pulvinar deorum
      tempus erat dapibus, sodales.
antehac nefas depromere Caecubum   5
   cellis avitis, dum Capitolio

1 **bibendum: bibo, bibere, bibi,** drink; (impersonal use of the gerundive) "Now we must drink …"
    libero: liber-libera-liberum, *adj.,* free; note *Liber* is another name for Bacchus, perhaps an intended pun; the word may also suggest the idea of freedom from fear of the enemy.

2 **pulsanda: pulso, pulsare, pulsavi, pulsatum,** beat, strike (in the dance)
    tellus: tellus, telluris, *f.,* earth
    Saliaribus: Saliaris-Saliare, *adj.,* of the Salii, priests of Mars

3 **ornare: orno, ornare, ornavi, ornatum,** decorate, adorn
    pulvinar: pulvinar, pulvinaris, *n.,* couch; the *pulvinaria* were the couches on which the images of the gods were placed and food set before them

4 **dapibus: daps, dapis,** *f.,* feast; the banquets of the Salii were famous for their sumptuousness
    sodales: sodalis, sodalis, *m.,* comrade

5 **antehac: antehac,** *adv.,* previously
    nefas: nefas, *n.,* (indeclinable) that which is wrong; supply *erat,* "it was wrong."
    depromere: depromo, depromere, deprompsi, depromptum, bring out
    Caecubum: Caecubum, Caecubi, *n.,* Caecuban wine (an expensive wine)

6 **cella: cella, cellae,** *f.,* storeroom, wine cellar
    avitis: avitus, -a, -um, *adj.,* ancestral
    Capitolio: Capitolium, Capitoli(i), *n.,* the Capitoline Hill (symbol of Rome)

7 **dementis: demens, dementis,** *adj.,* mad (an epithet transferred from *regina* to *ruinas*
    ruinas: ruina, ruinae, *f.,* ruin

8 **funus: funus, funeris,** *n.,* funeral, destruction; translate *et* before *funus.*

9 **contaminato: contaminatus, -a, -um,** *adj.,* polluted; this alludes to the eunuchs of Cleopatra's court.
    grege: grex, gregis, *m.,* herd
    turpium: turpis-turpe, *adj.,* filthy, foul

10 **morbo: morbus, morbi,** *m.,* disease
    quidlibet: quilibet, quaelibet, quidlibet, *pron.,* anyone, anything (any scheme of conquest)
    impotens: impotens, impotentis, *adj.,* uncontrolled, mad enough to

11 **sperare: spero, sperare, speravi, speratum,** hope for

12 **ebria: ebrius, -a, -um,** *adj.,* drunk
    minuit: minuo, minuere, minui, minutum, lessen, diminish
    furorem: furor, furoris, *m.,* fury, frenzy

13 **vix: vix,** *adv.,* scarcely
    sospes: sospes, sospitis, *adj.,* safe
    ignibus: ignis, ignis, *m.,* fire; fire broke out among the ships of Antony and destroyed them. Cleopatra escaped with sixty ships. Horace employs hyperbole on this occasion.

14 **lymphatam: lymphatus, -a, -um,** *adj.,* maddened, intoxicated
    Mareotico: Mareoticus, -a, -um, *adj.,* Mareotic (wine), grown around Lake Marea near Alexandria; *vino* is understood.

15 **redegit: redigo, redigere, redegi, redactum,** restore (to a former situation)
    veros: verus, -a, -um, *adj.,* genuine
    timor: timor, timoris, *m.,* fear

16 **Caesar: Caesar, Caesaris,** *m.,* Caesar Augustus
    Italia: Italia, Italiae, *f.,* Italy; Horace emphasizes that Augustus forced Cleopatra to go away from Italy *(ab Italia)* when she expressly intended to go to Italy *(ad Italiam);* he compelled her to go in the opposite direction.
    volantem: volo, volare, volavi, volatum, fly, rush

17 **remis: remus, remi,** *m.,* oar, (figuratively) galley
    adurgens: adurgeo, adurgere, adursi, press closely, pursue
    accipiter: accipiter, accipitris, *m.,* hawk
    velut: velut, *conj.,* just as

regina dementis ruinas
    funus et imperio parabat
contaminato cum grege turpium
morbo virorum, quidlibet impotens   10
    sperare fortunaque dulci
        ebria. sed minuit furorem
vix una sospes navis ab ignibus,
mentemque lymphatam Mareotico
    redegit in veros timores   15
        Caesar ab Italia volantem
remis adurgens, accipiter velut
mollis columbas aut leporem citus
    venator in campis nivalis
        Haemoniae, daret ut catenis   20
fatale monstrum; quae generosius
perire quaerens nec muliebriter

18 **mollis: mollis-molle,** *adj.,* gentle
   columbas: columba, columbae, *f.,* dove
   leporem: lepus, leporis, *m.,* hare
   citus: citus, -a, -um, *adj.,* swift

19 **venator: venator, venatoris,** *m.,* hunter
   campis: campus, campi, *m.,* plain
   nivalis: nivalis-nivale, *adj.,* snowy

20 **Haemoniae: Haemonia, Haemoniae,** *f.,* Haemonia, the old name for Thessaly in
      northern Greece
   catenis: catena, catenae, *f.,* chain; with *dare* the meaning is to put in chains with the
      purpose of exhibiting her in his triumphal parade in *Rome,* and then putting
      her to death

21 **fatale: fatalis-fatale,** *adj.,* deadly
   monstrum: monstrum, monstri, *n.,* monster (Cleopatra)
   quae: the antecedent should be the neuter *fatale monstrum*; but Horace is thinking
      of the sense more than of the grammar here.
   generosius: *comp. adv.,* derived from *generosus, -a, -um, adj.,* noble; the poet at
      this point grudgingly recognizes her heroic death as she boldly held the serpents
      close to her rather than to endure the triumph of Augustus.

22 **perire: pereo, perire, perii, peritum,** die, perish
   quaerens: quaero, quaerere, quaesivi, quaesitum, seek
   muliebriter: muliebriter, *adv.,* like a woman

23 **expavit: expavesco, expavescere, expavi,** dread
   ensem: ensis, ensis, *m.,* sword
   latentis: latens, latentis, *adj.,* hidden (modifies *oras*)

24 **classe: classis, classis,** *f.,* fleet
   cita: citus, -a, -um, *adj.,* swift
   reparavit: reparo, reparare, reparavi, reparatum, seek (in exchange for her palace)
   oras: ora, orae, *f.,* shore

25 **ausa: audeo, audere, ausus sum,** dare
   iacentem: iacens, iacentis, fallen, ruined
   visere: viso, visere, visi, visum, look at with attention, view
   regiam: regia, regiae, *f.,* palace

26 **vultu: vultus, vultus,** *m.,* expression (in the face)
   sereno: serenus, -a, -um, *adj.,* serene
   fortis: fortis-forte, *adj.,* brave, courageous (modifies the implied subject Cleopatra)
   asperas: asper, aspera, asperum, *adj.,* fierce, rough

27 **tractare: tracto, tractare, tractavi, tractatum,** handle; (with *fortis*) "brave enough to handle"
   serpentis: serpens, serpentis, *f.,* snake
   atrum: ater-atra-atrum, *adj.,* black; death *(mors)* is often described as black *(atra)*, hence deadly poison.

28 **combiberet: combibo, combibere, combibi,** drink in, absorb
   venenum: venenum, veneni, *n.,* poison

29 **deliberata: delibero, deliberare, deliberavi, deliberatum,** resolve
   ferocior: *comp. adj.* from *ferox, ferocis, adj.,* fierce, fierce-spirited, defiant; "becoming more defiant as she resolved to die"

30 **saevis: saevus, -a, -um,** *adj.,* hostile
   Liburnis: Liburna, Liburnae, *f.,* a light war vessel, similar to ships of the Liburnians of the Adriatic Sea, which figured prominently in Octavian's victory at Actium; understood is *classibus* or *navibus* to indicate the means by which Cleopatra would be led to the triumph in Rome.
   scilicet: scilicet, *adv.,* assuredly, of course
   invidens: invideo, invidere, invidi, invisum, begrudge, scorn; the infinitive *deduci* depends on *invidens.*

expavit ensem nec latentis
    classe cita reparavit oras;
ausa et iacentem visere regiam   25
vultu sereno, fortis et asperas
    tractare serpentis, ut atrum
        corpore combiberet venenum,
deliberata morte ferocior,
saevis Liburnis scilicet invidens   30
    privata deduci superbo
        non humilis mulier triumpho.

31 **privata: privatus, -a, -um,** *adj.,* of or belonging to a private individual; no longer a queen, Cleopatra is identified by the poet as a mere citizen.
    deduci: deduco, deducere, deduxi, deductum, conduct, lead, escort; refers to being led as a captured enemy in a triumphal parade in Rome
    superbo: superbus, -a, -um, *adj.,* proud

32 **humilis: humilis-humile,** *adj.,* submissive, humble
    triumpho: triumphus, triumphi, *m.,* triumph

Odes I.38

1   **Persicos: Persicus, -a, -um,** *adj.,* Persian, oriental
    puer: this is the standard word the Romans used to address a slave, whether a youth
        or an adult.
    apparatus: apparatus, apparatus, *m.,* luxury

2   **displicent: displiceo, displicere, displicui, displicitum,** displease
    nexae: necto, nectere, nexi, nexum, weave
    philyra: philyra, philyrae, *f.,* linden bark; *philyra* is an ablative of place where,
        since the garlands are woven onto a strip of linden bark
    coronae: corona, coronae, *f.,* garland; the Romans observed the peculiar custom
        of wearing garlands of flowers on their heads at dinner parties.

3   **sectari: sector, sectari, sectatus sum,** seek eagerly; with *mitte* the sense is *noli*
        followed by the infinitive *sectari.*
    rosa: rosa, rosae, *f.,* rose
    quo locorum = quibus locis (ablative of place where)

4   **sera: serus, -a, -um,** *adj.,* late
    moretur: moror, morari, moratus sum, linger

5   **simplici: simplex, simplicis,** *adj.,* simple, plain
    myrto: myrtus, myrti, *f.,* myrtle (here symbolic of less costly garlands)
    allabores: allaboro, allaborare, allaboravi, allaboratum, add to, embellish;
        subjunctive mood in a substantive clause introduced by *curo* with *ut* understood:
        "I would not have you add anything." *Ut* is sometimes omitted when it can easily
        be inferred from the dependent subjunctive.

6   **sedulus: sedulus, -a, -um,** *adj.,* attentive to detail; modifies the subject of *allabores*
        and has an adverbial force; painstakingly
    curo: curo, curare, curavi, curatum, care
    ministrum: minister, ministri, *m.,* servant, (in the context of dining) waiter; "as
        you serve the wine"

7   **dedecet: dedecet, dedecere, dedecuit,** it is unfitting
    arta: artus, -a, -um, *adj.,* dense, with leaves tightly packed together to afford
        shade

8   **vite: vitis, vitis,** *f.,* vine (poetic singular for plural)
    sub arta vite = under a grape arbor
    bibentem: bibo, bibere, bibi, drink

Horace is about to recline at dinner and addresses his attendant with a request for simplicity. It is possible that Horace may be expressing happiness with his accomplishment, namely the composition of Book I of the *Odes*, although there is nothing in the poem which alludes to this. However in this moment of celebration he rejects the eastern ornamental crowns, with their exotic weaving and their choice flowers, in favor of the simplicity which the poet's crown of myrtle (ivy) symbolizes. This poem's theme of simplicity contrasts with the grandeur of the last poem in Book III (*Odes* III.30), which predicts the immortality of the poet. The meter is Sapphic as in *Odes* I.10.

Persicos odi, puer, apparatus,
displicent nexae philyra coronae;
mitte sectari, rosa quo locorum
    sera moretur.
simplici myrto nihil allabores   5
sedulus curo: neque te ministrum
dedecet myrtus neque me sub arta
    vite bibentem.

The photograph captures a view of trees cropped so that they seem to join together. Notice how fully joined are the trees behind them. These are on the Janiculum Hill in the garden of the Villa Aurelia of the American Academy in Rome. *Odes* II.3. 9-11 refers to a similar conjunction.

Odes II.3   Saphic

Horace affirms for Dellius the need for all people to preserve a balanced attitude in good times and in bad, whether their lives have been forever sad or happy with self-indulgence. The poplar tree and pine tree, the brook with its counterflow exemplify the need for balance in action and in attitude. The ode sounds very Epicurean, particularly when the poet orders perfumes and flowers to be brought forth as long as fate permits. The mutability of life, as sounded earlier in *Odes* I.11 and 34, again causes Horace to think of the inevitability of departure from this world; poor and rich alike on the same boat are bound for the same port. The balanced images and parallel phrasing of the poem embody Horace's advice to maintain a balance in life. The meter is Alcaic as in *Odes* I.9

> fut, imperative
> Aequam memento rebus in arduis
> servare mentem, non secus in bonis adv
> ab insolenti temperatam
> laetitia, moriture Delli, abl separation
> fut act
> part

1   **aequam: aequus, -a, -um,** *adj.,* even, balanced, level
     memento: memini, meminisse, remember
     rebus: res, rei, *f.,* circumstance(s), situation
     arduis: arduus, -a, -um, *adj.,* difficult, steep

2   **servare: servo, servare, servavi, servatum,** keep
     mentem: mens, mentis, *f.,* mind; (level) head
     non secus: non secus, *adv.,* not otherwise, just as; an example of asyndeton and
          litotes

3   **insolenti: insolens, insolentis,** *adj.,* excessive, unusual
     temperatam: tempero, temperare, temperavi, temperatum, (with *ab*) restrain
          from, refrain from

4   **laetitia: laetitia, laetitiae,** *f.,* joy
     moriture: morior, mori, mortuus sum, die; the future participle is best translated
          "destined to die someday"
     Delli: Dellius, Delli(i), *m.,* Dellius, friend of Antony who deserted to Augustus;
          he changed sides in the civil wars so frequently that he was called *desultor
          bellorum civilium,* one who leapt from horse to horse in the circus; as a military
          and political veteran, Dellius is an example of a person whose survival depended
          upon his maintenance of a distinguished equilibrium at all times, the basic point
          of the poem.

5   **seu … seu** = whether … or
     maestus: maestus, -a, -um, *adj.,* sad (used here with adverbial force)
     vixeris: vivo, vivere, vixi, victum, live; *vixeris* is future perfect indicative
     omni tempore: ablative, duration of time

6   **remoto: remotus, -a, -um,** *adj.,* secluded
     gramine: gramen, graminis, *n.,* grass, grassy spot

7   **festos: festus, -a, -um,** *adj.,* festive
     per festos dies = throughout the holidays
     reclinatum: reclinatus, -a, -um, *adj.,* reclining, having reclined
     bearis = beaveris: beo, beare, beavi, beatum, make happy; *bearis* is also a
          syncopated future perfect indicative

8   **interiore: interior-interius,** *adj.,* inner, (figuratively) choice; older bottles of wine
          were stored deeper inside the wine cellar.
     nota: nota, notae, *f.,* mark, vintage; the various amphoras containing wine were
          labeled with the names of the consuls for that year.
     Falerni: Falernum, Falerni, *n.,* Falernian, a very good wine from the Ager Falernus
          near Mount Massicus in Campania

9   **quo: quo,** *adv.,* why; **pinus: pinus, pini,** *f.,* pine (a dark, massive tree)
     ingens: ingens, ingentis, *adj.,* huge, mighty, tall
     albaque: albus, -a, -um, *adj.,* white
     populus: populus, populi, *f.,* poplar

10   **umbram: umbra, umbrae,** *f.,* shade
     hospitalem: hospitalis-hospitale, *adj.,* friendly, hospitable
     consociare: consocio, consociare, consociavi, consociatum, entwine, join

11   **quid: quid,** *adv.,* why (like *quo* in line 9 above)
     ramis: ramus, rami, *m.,* branch
     obliquo: obliquus, -a, -um, *adj.,* winding
     laborat: laboro, laborare, laboravi, laboratum, strive, struggle

12   **lympha: lympha, lymphae,** *f.,* clear water
     fugax: fugax, fugacis, *adj.,* hurrying
     trepidare: trepido, trepidare, trepidavi, trepidatum, rush along; "ripple"
     rivo: rivus, rivi, *m.,* course, channel; "winding course"

13   **huc: huc,** *adv.,* hither, to this place
     unguenta: unguentum, unguenti, *n.,* perfume
     nimium: nimium, *adv.,* too much, (with adjectives and adverbs) too
     nimium brevis-nimium breves = too short-lived

seu maestus omni tempore vixeris;   5

seu te in remoto gramine per dies
    festos reclinatum bearis
        interiore nota Falerni.

quo pinus ingens albaque populus
umbram hospitalem consociare amant   10
    ramis? quid obliquo laborat
        lympha fugax trepidare rivo?

huc vina et unguenta et nimium brevis
flores amoenae ferre iube rosae,
    dum res et aetas et sororum   15
        fila trium patiuntur atra.

cedes coemptis saltibus et domo
villaque flavus quam Tiberis lavit;
    cedes, et exstructis in altum

---

14 **flores: flos, floris,** *m.,* flower
    amoenae: amoenus, -a, -um, *adj.,* pleasant, lovely
    ferre: fero, ferre, tuli, latum, bring
    iube: iubeo, iubere, iussi, iussum, order, bid; *servos* or *ministros* is understood
        after *iube.*

15 **res: res, rei,** *f.,* circumstances, (financial) resources
    aetas: aetas, aetatis, *f.,* age, youth, time
    sororum: soror, sororis, *f.,* sister; this refers to the three fates, Clotho (the spinner
        of the thread of life), Lachesis (the measurer of the thread of life) and Atropos
        (the one who cuts the thread of life).

16 **fila: filum, fili,** *n.,* thread
    patiuntur: patior, pati, passus sum, allow, permit
    atra: ater-atra-atrum, *adj.,* black (because the cutting of the thread of life brings
        death)

17 **cedes: cedo, cedere, cessi, cessum,** leave, depart
    coemptis: coemo, coemere, coemi, coemptum, buy up; the word implies that land
        was bought up in one small pasture after another.
    saltibus: saltus, saltus, *m.,* mountain pasture

18 **flavus: flavus, -a, -um,** *adj.,* yellow, (perhaps) sandy colored
    lavit: lavo, lavere, lavi, lautum, wash

19 **exstructis: exstruo, exstruere, exstruxi, exstructum,** heap up

20 **divitiis: divitiae, divitiarum,** *f. pl.,* riches
    potietur: potior, potiri, potitus sum, (with the ablative case) gain possession of, become master of
    heres: heres, heredis, *m.,* heir

21 **divesne: dives, divitis,** *adj.,* rich
    prisco: priscus, -a, -um, *adj.,* ancient
    natus: nascor, nasci, natus sum, be born
    Inacho: Inachus, Inachi, *m,,* Inachus, a mythical first king of Argos and therefore suggestive of ancient lineage

22 **interest: intersum, interesse, interfui,** (used impersonally) it makes a difference; (with *nil)* it makes no difference
    pauper: pauper, pauperis, *adj.,* poor
    infima: infimus, -a, -um, *adj.,* lowly

23 **divo: divus, -a, -um,** *adj.,* divine; *sub divo* is an idiomatic phrase meaning under the sky, in the open.
    moreris: moror, morari, moratus sum, (poetic equivalent of *vivo)* live, dwell; Horace suggests that life is temporary, a sojourn; the verb *moror* and *commoror* are commonly used to suggest staying in place for a short while, e.g., at an inn.

24   **miserantis: miseror, miserari, miseratus sum,** pity
    Orci: Orcus, Orci, *m.,* Orcus, god of the lower world

25 **eodem: eodem,** *adv.,* to the same place
    cogimur: cogo, cogere, coegi, coactum, gather, herd (the technical word for the gathering of the flock)

26 **versatur: verso, versare, versavi, versatum,** turn, shake up
    urna: urna, urnae, *f.,* urn
    serius: serius, *adv.* , later
    ocius: ocius, *adv.,* sooner

27 **sors: sors, sortis,** *f.,* lot
    exitura: exeo, exire, exii, exitum, fly out; this word elides with *et* as does *aeternum* with *exsilium,* which also elides with *impositura.* The pronounced elisions in this line convey the image of an unbreakable chain of events which binds all human beings to this fate.
    aeternum exsilium: these are accusatives object of the preposition *in* after a verb of sending or journeying to express a destination

divitiis potietur heres. *abl with verb*   20
divesne prisco natus ab Inacho
nil interest an pauper et infima
    de gente sub divo moreris, *dep pres subj unc* *act* *ind*
        victima nil *miserantis* Orci. *pres act part*
omnes eodem cogimur, omnium   25
versatur urna serius ocius
    sors exitura et nos in aeternum *fut act part*
        exsilium impositura cumbae.

boat of Cheron

28 **impositura: impono, imponere, imposui, impositum,** (with dative) place in, place
    upon
  cumbae: cumba, cumbae, *f.,* skiff, little boat; the boat used by Charon to ferry the
    souls of the dead across the river Styx. How does the feeling at the close of the
    poem connect with the spirit of the opening lines?

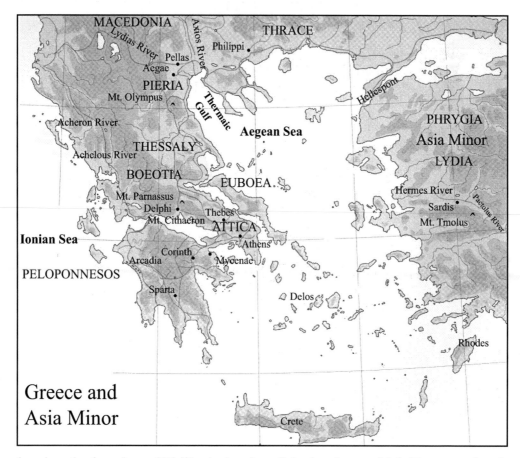

Map showing the location of Philippi, the site of the battle to which Horace refers in *Odes* II.7

Odes II.7

Surprised to see Pompeius, a friend he last saw on the battlefield of Philippi in November, 42 B.C., Horace recalls their good times together in the past as well as their parting on the field of battle. Pompeius is urged to make suitable votive offerings to express gratitude to the gods who saved his life. Horace uses this unexpected moment not to express spontaneous joy like that of Catullus 9, but to comment humorously on his own performance as a soldier. He echoes the Greek lyric poet Archilochus, who describes the loss of his shield in battle, and reinforces for the reader his own claim to be chief among the poets to bring Greek song to Italian meters (*Odes* III.30.13-14). The meter is Alcaic as in I.9 and II.3.

> O saepe mecum tempus in ultimum
> deducte Bruto militiae duce,
>   quis te redonavit Quiritem
>   dis patriis Italoque caelo,
> Pompei, meorum prime sodalium?   5
> cum quo morantem saepe diem mero

1   **saepe: saepe,** *adv.,* often; there were many engagements before the decisive battle
    ultimum: ultimus, -a, -um, *adj.,* extreme; with *tempus* there is the sense of peril or danger

2   **deducte: deduco, deducere, deduxi, deductum,** lead
    Bruto: Brutus, Bruti, *m.,* Brutus, the general at Philippi; an ablative absolute with *duce* and *militiae* dependent upon *duce;* at the time of this battle (42 B.C.) Horace was on the side of those opposed to Octavian.

3   **redonavit: redono, redonare, redonavi, redonatum,** restore; this word was invented by Horace.
    Quiritem: Quiris, Quiritis, *m.,* a Roman citizen (with full civil rights; the term implies civilian status)

4   **patriis: patrius, -a, -um.,** *adj.,* of your country
    caelo: caelum, caeli, *n.,* sky, climate; perhaps in contrast to that of Philippi

5   **Pompei: Pompeius, Pompei(i),** *m.,* Pompey, comrade-in-arms of Horace at Philippi, not the Pompeius who was a triumvir
    primus: primus, -a, -um, *adj.,* first; here there is the sense of my "best" friend
    sodalium: sodalis, sodalis, *m.,* companion, "army buddy"

6   **morantem: moror, morari, moratus sum,** pass slowly, drag on
    mero: merum, meri, *n.,* wine unmixed with water

7   **fregi: frango, frangere, fregi, fractum,** break up, while away
    coronatus: corono, coronare, coronavi, coronatum, crown, wreathe
    nitentis: niteo, nitere, nitui, glisten

8   **malobathro: malobathrum, malobathri,** *n.,* perfume; depends on *nitentis* which
       modifies *capillos.*
    capillos: capillus, capilli, *m.,* hair; an accusative of respect with *coronatus*

9   **Philippos: Philippi, Philipporum,** *m. pl.,* a city in Thrace (see map) where Brutus
       and Cassius were defeated in 42 B.C.

10 **sensi: sentio, sentire, sensi, sensum,** experience
    relicta: relinquo, relinquere, reliqui, relictum, leave, abandon
    non bene = disgracefully
    parmula: parmula, parmulae, *f.,* shield; this reference to the loss of his shield is
       symbolic more than factual; Horace is probably imitating a similar passage in
       the Greek lyric poet Archilochus; the Greeks called the loss of one's shield a
       ripsaspis; rips means "seize," *aspis* "shield."

11 **fracta: frango, frangere, fregi, fractum,** break; *est* is understood; "when valor
       reached the breaking point"
    virtus: virtus, virtutis, *f.,* courage, valor
    minaces: minax, minacis, *adj.,* threatening, menacing; *milites* is understood.

12 **turpe: turpis-turpe,** *adj.,* ignoble; in sense this word aligns with *tetigere,* although
       it modifies *solum.*
    solum: solum, soli, *n.,* ground
    tetigere: tango, tangere, tetigi, tactum, touch; *tetigere = tetigerunt*
    mento: mentum, menti, *n.,* chin (poetic singular); "Soldiers till then so threatening
       ignobly bit the dust."

13 **Mercurius: Mercurius, Mercuri(i),** *m.,* Mercury, messenger of the gods and patron
       of poets
    celer: celer, celeris, celere, *adj.,* (with adverbial force) quick, speedy

14 **paventem: paveo, pavere, pavi,** quake with fear, tremble
    sustulit: tollo, tollere, sustuli, sublatum, bear off, carry away
    aere: aer, aeris, *m.,* fog, mist; Horace is here satirizing Homer, who at times
       represents divinities rescuing downed heroes.

15 **rursus: rursus,** *adv.,* again
    in bellum: to be taken with both *resorbens* and *tulit*
    resorbens: resorbeo, resorbere, pull back, draw back (in); the metaphor is from
       a shipwreck: the waves had carried Horace safely to shore, but the undertow
       had sucked his friend back "on troubled water," probably the continued service
       under Sextus Pompeius.

fregi coronatus nitentis
    malobathro Syrio capillos. *acc of respect*
tecum Philippos et celerem fugam
sensi relicta non bene parmula, *ablabls* *perf pass part*   10
    cum fracta virtus, et minaces
      turpe solum tetigere mento. *perf act ind 3pl*
sed me per hostis Mercurius celer

dense mist literally surrounds quaking person (Horace)

denso paventem sustulit aere; *abl means*
    te rursus in bellum resorbens *pres act part.* 15
      unda fretis tulit aestuosis. *abl means*
ergo obligatam redde Iovi dapem
longaque fessum militia latus
    depone sub lauru mea, nec *dat ref*
      parce cadis tibi destinatis. *abl w*   20
oblivioso levia Massico

16 **unda: unda, undae,** *f.,* wave
    fretis: fretum, freti, *n.,* sea, surf
    aestuosis: aestuosus, -a, -um, *adj.,* raging, troubled, seething

17 **ergo: ergo,** *adv.,* therefore
    obligatam: obligo, obligare, obligavi, obligatum, pledge, owe
    redde: reddo, reddere, reddidi, redditum, render, give in return (for your
        preservation)
    dapem: daps, dapis, *f.,* banquet, feast

18 **militia: militia, militiae,** *f.,* military service
    latus: latus, lateris, *n.,* flank, side; (figuratively) body

19 **depone: depono, deponere, deposui, depositum,** put down, lay down
    lauru: laurus, laurus, *f.,* laurel tree

20 **parce: parco, parcere, peperci, parsum,** spare, refrain from
    cadis: cadus, cadi, *m.,* wine jar
    destinatis: destino, destinare, destinavi, destinatum, select, set apart; "meant for
        you"

21 **levis: levis-leve,** *adj.,* polished, smooth
    oblivioso: obliviosus, -a, -um, *adj.,* causing forgetfulness
    Massico: Massicus, Massici, *m.,* Massic, a wine produced in Campania near Mount
        Massicus

22 **ciboria: ciborium, cibori(i), *n.,*** goblet
    exple: expleo,, explere, explevi, expletum, fill up, fill to the brim
    funde: fundo, fundere, fudi, fusum, pour out
    capacibus: capax, capacis, *adj.,* capacious, full

23 **unguenta: unguentum, unguenti, *n.,*** perfume
    conchis: concha, conchae, *f.,* shell-shaped vessel, conch
    udo: udus, -a, -um, *adj.,* moist, pliant

24 **deproperare: depropero, deproperare, deproperavi, deproperatum,** prepare
    speedily, weave fast
    apio: apium, api(i), *n.,* parsley; parsley was used by the Greeks to make garlands
    to be given out as prizes at the Nemean games; Romans also used it to make
    garlands.

25 **curatve:** the enclitic *-ve* would be attached to *myrto* in prose; here it is attached to
    curat but should be translated with *myrto.*
    Venus is an ambiguous allusion to the highest dice-throw, when the four upturned
    faces are each different.
    arbitrum: arbiter, arbitri, *m.,* master, master of ceremonies; the Romans followed
    a custom of choosing by lot an *arbiter bibendi* to administer and supervise a
    ceremony.

26 **dicet: dico, dicere, dixi, dictum,** name, appoint
    sanius: *comp. adv.,* from *sanus, -a, -um, adj.,* sane, sensible; *non sanius* is litotes
    for *insanius,* "more wildly than …"

27 **bacchabor: bacchor, bacchari, bacchatus sum,** revel
    Edonis: Edoni, Edonorum, *m. pl.,* Edonians (ablative of comparison), a Thracian
    people known for their frenzied worship of Bacchus
    recepto: recipio, recipere, recepi, receptum, regain

28 **dulce: dulcis-dulce, *adj.,*** nice, enjoyable
    furere: furo, furere, carouse, revel

ciboria exple; funde capacibus
    unguenta de conchis. quis udo
       deproperare apio coronas
curatve myrto? quem Venus arbitrum   25
dicet bibendi? non ego sanius
    bacchabor Edonis: recepto
       dulce mihi furere est amico.

Odes II.10

1   **rectius:** *comp. adv.* from *rectus, -a, -um, adj.,* upright, correct, proper; "you will live a better life."

    Licini: Licinius, Licini(i), *m.,* Licinius, adopted brother of Maecenas' wife, Terentia; Licinius Murena was also adopted by Aulus Terentius Varro and executed in 22 B.C. for his involvement in a conspiracy against Augustus.

    altum: altum, alti, *n.,* the deep sea

2   **urgendo: urgeo, urgere, ursi,** press upon; (figuratively) sail

    procellas: procella, procellae, *f.,* gale, squall, storm

3   **cautus: cautus, -a, -um,** *adj.,* cautious

    horrescis: horresco, horrescere, horrui, dread, become terrified at

    nimium: nimium, *adv.,* too much

    premendo: premo, premere, pressi, pressum, bear down upon, stay close to, hug (the shore)

4   **litus: litus, litoris,** *n.,* shore

    iniquum: iniquus, -a, -um, *adj.,* uneven, dangerous

5   **quisque: quisquis-quidquid,** *pron.,* whoever

    auream: aureus, -a, -um, *adj.,* golden

    mediocritatem: mediocritas, mediocritatis, *f.,* moderation

6   **diligit: diligo, diligere, dilexi, dilectum,** prize

    tutus: tutus, -a, -um, *adj.,* safe (used adverbially)

    caret: careo, carere, carui, caritum, be without, be free from (with ablative), avoids

    obsoleti: obsoletus, -a, -um, *adj.,* shabby, dilapidated, run-down

7   **sordibus: sordes, sordis,** *f.,* dirt, filth

    tecti: tectum, tecti, *n.,* roof, (by synecdoche) house; note the asyndeton and anaphora.

    invidenda: invideo, invidere, invidi, invisum, envy

8   **sobrius: sobrius, -a, -um,** *adj.,* prudent (used adverbially)

    aula: aula, aulae, *f.,* mansion, palace

9   **saepius: saepius,** *adv.,* more often

    agitatur: agito, agitare, agitavi, agitatum, shake

10 **ingens: ingens, ingentis,** *adj.,* tall, huge, towering

    pinus: pinus, pini, *f.,* pine tree

    celsae: celsus, -a, -um, *adj.,* lofty

    graviore: gravus, -a, -um, *adj.,* heavy

  casu: casus, casus, *m.,* fall, crash

Odes II.10

In giving advice to Maecenas' brother-in-law Licinius, Horace extols the golden mean. The advice recalls *Odes* II.3 and, in part, *Odes* I.34. Sailing over wind-tossed seas makes it necessary to steer a careful course. This exhortation in the poem's opening and closing stanzas also embodies the theme in *Odes* I.11.6-7. Horace gives examples of the dangers posed by extremes of various sorts in order to emphasize the need to steer a middle course in all of life's situations: the massive pine tree is shaken by the winds; huge towers fall with a louder crash; lightning hits the tops of mountains. Man's heart must be prepared for change, a constant observed by and in nature; Apollo sings as well as stings. The meter is Sapphic, as in *Odes* I.10.

Rectius vives, Licini, neque altum
semper urgendo neque, dum procellas
cautus horrescis, nimium premendo
    litus iniquum.

auream quisquis mediocritatem   5
diligit, tutus caret obsoleti
sordibus tecti, caret invidenda
    sobrius aula.

saepius ventis agitatur ingens
pinus et celsae graviore casu   10
decidunt turres feriuntque summos
    fulgura montis.

sperat infestis, metuit secundis
alteram sortem bene praeparatum

11 **decidunt: decido, decidere, decidi,** topple
   turres: turris, turris, *f.,* tower
   feriuntque: ferio, ferire, strike

12 **fulgura: fulgur, fulguris,** *n.,* lightning

13 **infestis: infestus, -a, -um,** *adj.,* disturbed, dangerous, adverse, (used substantively) in adversity (ablative of circumstance)
   metuit: metuo, metuere, metui, fear
   secundis: secundus, -a, -um, *adj.,* favorable, prosperous, (used substantively) in prosperity (ablative of circumstance)

14 **sortem: sors, sortis,** *f.,* lot

> pectus. informis hiemes reducit   15
>   Iuppiter, idem
> summovet. non, si male nunc, et olim
> sic erit: quondam cithara tacentem
> suscitat Musam neque semper arcum
>   tendit Apollo.   20
>   rebus angustis animosus atque
> fortis appare; sapienter idem
> contrahes vento nimiumn secundo
>   turgida vela.

[Handwritten annotations: "accdo" above hiemes; "abl means" after tacentem; "abl circumstance" after tendit Apollo; "Nautical image: furling the sail to windy=bad" bracketing lines 21–24; "adv" after idem; "accdo" after vela.]

15 **pectus: pectus, pectoris,** *n.,* chest, heart
informis: informis-informe, *adj.,* hideous, nasty
hiemes: hiems, hiemis, *f.,* winter
reducit = bring back (year after year)

16 **idem: idem, eadem, idem,** *adj.,* the same; here used adverbially, "likewise"

17 **summovet: summoveo, summovere, summovi, summotum,** take away, remove
si male: supply *est;* **olim: olim,** adv., someday

18 **quondam: quondam,** *adv.,* (a rare meaning) sometimes
cithara: cithara, citharae, *f.,* lyre (ablative of means)
tacentem: taceo, tacere, tacui, tacitum, be silent

19 **suscitat: suscito, suscitare, suscitavi, suscitatum,** wake, awake; Apollo is the
subject of *suscitat* and *tendit.*
arcum: arcus, arcus, *m.,* bow

20 **tendit: tendo, tendere, tetendi, tensum,** stretch

21 **angustis: angustus, -a, -um,** *adj.,* narrow; stressful, critical
animosus: animosus, -a, -um, *adj.,* bold

22 **appare: appareo, apparere, apparui, apparitum,** show oneself
sapienter: sapienter, *adv.,* wisely; "if you are wise"
idem, see line 16.

23 **contrahes: contraho, contrahere, contraxi, contractum,** furl, take in
nimium: nimium, *adv.,* too
secundo: secundus, -a, -um, *adj.,* favorable

24 **turgida: turgidus, -a, -um,** *adj.,* swollen; **vela: velum, veli,** *n.,* sail

Odes II.14

This poem, addressed to a certain Postumus, is an elaborate reflection on the inevitability of death. It emphasizes that goodness, religious devotion, and sacrifices to the gods do not alter what comes ultimately for rich and poor alike. Humankind's worry over war and weather is vain. Everyone must cross the river Styx on a journey; all must experience a separation from the material things which were once cherished as treasures, and which now constitute the inheritance of an uncaring heir. The meter is Alcaic as in *Odes* I.9.

> Eheu fugaces, Postume, Postume,
> labuntur anni nec pietas moram
> rugis et instanti senectae
> adferet indomitaeque morti:
> non si trecenis quotquot eunt dies,
> amice, places illacrimabilem
> Plutona tauris, qui ter amplum

1   **eheu: eheu,** (exclamation) alas!; **fugaces: fugax, fugacis,** *adj.,* fleeting
Postume: Postumus, Postumi, *m.,* Postumus, a man's name; this derives from *post,* after and *humus,* burial, i.e., after his father died

2   **labuntur: labor, labi, lapsus sum,** glide, slip by, slip away
pietas: pietas, pietatis, *f.,* loyalty, righteousness; this term covers all human responsibility both to the gods and to one's fellow man.
moram: mora, morae, *f.,* delay

3   **rugis: ruga, rugae,** *f.,* wrinkle
instanti: insto, instare, institi, press closely upon, threaten; "approaching"

4   **adferet: adfero, adferre, adtuli, allatum,** cause, bring
indomitaeque: indomitus, -a, -um, *adj.,* unsubdued, invincible

5   **trecenis: treceni-ae-a,** *adj.,* three-hundred at a time
quotquot: quotquot, (indeclinable) *adj.,* however many
eunt: eo, ire, ii, itum, go, go by
quotquot eunt dies = *cotidie*

6   **places: placo, placare, placavi, placatum,** appease, please
illacrimabilem: illacrimabilis-illacrimabile, *adj.,* without tears, pitiless

7   **Plutona: Pluto, Plutonis,** *m.,* Pluto, king of the underworld
tauris: taurus, tauri, *m.,* bull
amplum: amplus, -a, -um, *adj.,* large; *ter amplum,* "of triple frame"

8 **Geryonen: Geryon, Geryonis,** *m.,* Geryon, a giant with three bodies
   Tityonque: Tityos, Tityi, *m.,* Tityos, the giant who was punished in Hades for
        insulting Latona, mother of Apollo and Artemis (Diana)
   tristi: tristis-triste, *adj.,* sad, gloomy

9 **compescit: compesco, compescere, compescui,** restrain, imprison
   unda = stream (the Styx)
   scilicet: scilicet, *adv.,* certainly, of course
   omnibus: dative of agent with the gerundive *enaviganda*

10 **munere: munus, muneris,** *n.,* gift, bounty
   vescimur: vescor, vesci, eat, fill oneself with (with ablative), "live on"

11 **enaviganda: enavigo, enavigare, enavigavi, enavigatum,** (root verb *navigo*) cross,
        sail across; the prefix "e" adds the notion of "from one side to the other" or "to
        the farthur shore"; this is the gerundive form with *unda* in line 9 in the ablative,
        dependent upon *compescit* in line 9.
   reges: not so much kings but more the idea of princes, wealthy landlords

12 **inopes: inops, inopis,** *adj.,* needy, poor
   coloni: colonus, coloni, *m.,* farmer, sharecropper; the contrast is between land
        owners (*reges*) and tenant farmers (*coloni*).

13 **frustra: frustra,** *adv.,* in vain
   cruento: cruentus, -a, -um, *adj.,* bloody
   carebimus: careo, carere, carui, (with ablative) keep free from, escape

14 **fractisque: frango, frangere, fregi, fractum,** break
   rauci: raucus, -a, -um, *adj.,* coarse, rough
   fluctibus: fluctus, fluctus, *m.,* wave; *fractis fluctibus* = breakers
   Hadriae: Hadria, Hadriae, *f.,* the Adriatic Sea

15 **autumnos: autumnus, autumni,** *m.,* autumn; autumn was often spoken of as the
        most unhealthy season of the year because of the Sirocco (*Auster*) wind which
        blows from the Sahara in Africa.
   nocentem: noceo, nocere, nocui, harm (with dative)

16 **metuemus: metuo, metuere, metui,** fear
   Austrum: Auster, Austri, *m.,* the south wind

17 **visendus: viso, visere, visi, visum,** look at with attention
   flumine: flumen, fluminis, *n.,* river, "flow"
   languido: languidus, -a, -um, *adj.,* sluggish

Geryonen Tityonque tristi

compescit unda, scilicet omnibus,

quicumque terrae munere vescimur,   10

enaviganda, sive reges

sive inopes erimus coloni.

frustra cruento Marte carebimus

fractisque rauci fluctibus Hadriae,

frustra per autumnos nocentem   15

corporibus metuemus Austrum:

visendus ater flumine languido

Cocytos errans et Danai genus

infame damnatusque longi

Sisyphus Aeolides laboris: 20

linquenda tellus et domus et placens

uxor, neque harum quas colis arborum

---

18 **Cocytos: Cocytos, Cocyti,** *m.,* Cocytos, the river of mourning in the underworld

Danai: Danaus, Danai, *m.,* king whose daughters (except Hypermnestra) killed their husbands on their wedding night; in Hades the daughters must carry water in leaky buckets for eternity.

genus = offspring

19 **infame: infamis-infame,** *adj.,* infamous

damnatusque: damno, damnare, damnavi, damnatum, (with genitive of the charge) condemn to; "condemned to endless labor"

longi = ceaseless, endless

20 **Sisyphus: Sisyphus, Sisyphi,** *m.,* Sisyphus, the king of Corinth who because of his greed was forced to roll a stone uphill forever in Hades.

Aeolides: Aeolides, Aeolidae, *m.,* (a patronymic) son of Aeolus, namely, Sisyphus

21 **linquenda: linquo, linquere, liqui,** leave behind; the form recalls the sound of *enaviganda* in line 11 and *visendus* in line 17.

tellus: tellus, telluris, *f.,* land, earth

placens: placeo, placere, placui, placitum, please

22 **uxor: uxor, uxoris,** *f.,* wife

colis: colo, colere, colui, cultum, take care of, cultivate; raise

arborum: arbor, arboris, *f.,* tree

te praeter invisas cupressos *acc* *art*
  ulla brevem dominum sequetur: *3 fut ind*
absumet heres Caecuba dignior   25
  servata centum clavibus et mero   *w. her*
tinget pavimentum superbo,   *very expensive*
  pontificum potiore cenis. *abl comparison*

23 **praeter: praeter,** *prep.*, except (with accusative)
      invisas: invisus, -a, -um, *adj.*, hated
      cupressos: cupressus, cupressi, *f.*, the cypress tree; this was symbolic of death and
          was sacred to Pluto (Hades); hence it was often planted near cemeteries.

24 The *neque* of line 22 must be translated with *ulla* of line 24; understand *arbor* with
      ulla.
      brevem: brevis-breve, *adj.*, short-lived

25 **absumet: absumo, absumere, absumpsi, absumptum,** consume, drink up
      heres: heres, heredis, *m.*, heir
      Caecuba: Caecubum, Caecubi, *n.*, Caecuban wine
      dignior: *comp. adj.*, from *dignus, -a, -um, adj.*, worthy; this word has an ironic note
          since the heir both uses and enjoys the inherited wines.

26 **servata: servo, servare, servavi, servatum,** guard, protect
      clavibus: clavis, clavis, *f.*, key

27 **tinget: tinguo, tinguere, tinxi, tinctum,** stain; the reference to spilling precious
          wine on the pavement suggests the reckless extravagance of the heir.
      pavimentum: pavimentum, pavimenti, *n.*, pavement
      superbo: superbus, -a, -um, *adj.*, splendid, proud; modifies *mero* but in sense goes
          with the subject of *tinget.*

28 **pontificum: pontifex, pontificis,** *m.*, high priest; the feasts of the priestly boards
          or colleges, as they are called, were proverbial for their magnificence.
      potiore: potior-potius, *adj.*, better ("than the wine used at the banquets of …")
      cenis: cena, cenae, *f.*, dinner, banquet

Odes II.16

This ode, addressed to Grosphus, a Roman knight who owned large estates in Sicily, asserts the desire for tranquility and peace, which mankind requests in times of danger. Neither wealth nor power will buy inner peace of mind. No excesses, no travels, no military service, no halls can make a person free from anxiety. Simple living is the key to a successful, happy life, which can never be considered fortunate in every aspect. Being happy at the moment precludes anxiety over tomorrow. Neither young Achilles nor aged Tithonus escaped death. Finally for Horace, large herds of cattle and horses, extensive land holdings, and elaborate clothing pale in value when compared to the transcendent gift of writing lyric poetry. The meter is Sapphic, as in *Odes* I.10.

Otium divos rogat in patenti
prensus Aegaeo, simul atra nubes
condidit lunam neque certa fulgent
    sidera nautis;
otium bello furiosa Thrace,   5

1   **otium: otium, oti(i),** *n.,* peace, tranquility; compare and contrast Catullus' use of the word in 51.13-16, which is also written in Sapphic meter.
     patenti: patens, patentis, *adj.,* open

2   **prensus: prendo, prendere, prendi, prensum,** catch; (used substantively) "the mariner caught"
     Aegaeo: Aegaeum, Aegaei, *n.,* the Aegean Sea
     simul = simula atque (ac), *conj.,* as soon as
     nubes: nubes, nubis, *f.,* cloud

3   **condidit: condo, condere, condidi, conditum,** hide
     certa: certus, -a, -um, *adj.,* sure, dependable; *certa* should be taken predicatively, i.e. "shine sure with their trusty light"
     fulgent: fulgeo, fugere, fulsi, shine; note the contrast with *condidit.*

4   **sidera: sidus, sideris,** *n.,* constellation; since the compass had not yet been invented, the ancients depended on the constellations for navigating by night. They located the North by the Great Bear (Ursus Maior), seven stars of which form the Big Dipper

5   **furiosa: furiosus, -a, -um,** *adj.,* furious
     Thrace: Thrace, Thraces, *f.,* Thrace, east of Macedonia in northern Greece*Rogat* (line 1) is understood with *Thrace* and with *Medi* (line 6)

6   **Medi: Medus, Medi,** *m.,* Mede, Persian, Parthian

pharetra: pharetra, pharetrae, *f.,* quiver
decori: decorus, -a, -um, *adj.,* adorned

7   **Grosphe: Grosphus, Grosphi,** *m.,* Grosphus, a Roman knight
gemmis: gemma, gemmae, *f.,* gem
purpura: purpura, purpurae, *f.,* purple garment, symbol of wealth or authority

8   **ve-nale: venalis-venale,** *adj.,* able to be bought; joined with *neque* and modifies
otium.
auro: aurum, auri, *n.,* gold

9   **gazae: gaza, gazae,** *f.,* wealth
consularis: consularis-consulare, *adj.,* consular, consul's

10 **summovet: summoveo, summovere, summovi, summotum,** banish, move away;
this verb is used also in *Odes* II.10.17.
lictor: lictor, lictoris, *m.,* lictor, attendant who precedes the consul, making way
for him or moving the unruly crowds *(tumultus)* out of his way
tumultus: tumultus, tumultus, *m.,* tumult, turmoil

11 **mentis:** with this word there is a sudden shift from political to mental imagery.
laqueata: laqueatus, -a, -um, *adj.,* paneled, coffered; an expensive feature

12 **volantis: volo, volare, volavi, volatum,** flit; this word modifies *curas* of line 11.

13 **vivitur: vivo, vivere, vixi, victum,** live; (impersonal usage) "it is lived," "one
lives."
parvo: parvus, -a, -um, *adj.,* little; (used substantively) "a little" (ablative of
means)
cui: a dative of reference with the force of a possessive genitive, "on whose table"
paternum: paternus, -a, -um, *adj.,* ancestral; this word suggests tradition and
constancy.

14 **splendet: splendeo, splendere,** shine
mensa: mensa, mensae, *f.,* table
tenui: tenuis-tenue, *adj.,* modest, frugal
salinum: salinum, salini, *n.,* salt shaker; the idea here is that the only costly piece
of tableware is this hand-me-down.

15 **levis: levis-leve,** *adj.,* gentle; the form is accusative plural and modifies *somnos.*
timor: timor, timoris, *m.,* fear (of loss)
cupido: cupido, cupidinis, *m.,* desire (for gain); modified by *sordidus* = greed

otium Medi pharetra decori,
Grosphe, non gemmis neque purpura ve-
   nale neque auro.
non enim gazae neque consularis
summovet lictor miseros tumultus   10
mentis et curas laqueata circum
   tecta volantis.
vivitur parvo bene, cui paternum
splendet in mensa tenui salinum
nec levis somnos timor aut cupido   15
   sordidus aufert.
quid brevi fortes iaculamur aevo
multa? quid terras alio calentis
sole mutamus? patriae quis exsul
   se quoque fugit?   20
scandit aeratas vitiosa navis

16 **sordidus: sordidus, -a, -um,** *adj.,* vulgar, foul
   aufert: aufero, auferre, abstuli, ablatum, take away, spoil

17 **quid: quid,** *adv.,* why
   fortes modifies the implied subject of *iaculamur* and has an adverbial force,
      "undauntedly"
   iaculamur: iaculor, iaculari, iaculatus sum, strive after
   aevo: aevum, aevi, *n.,* life, lifetime

18 **multa: multus, -a, -um,** *adj.,* much, (pl.) many; (used substantively) "many
      possessions"; **quid: quid,** *adv.,* why
   calentis: caleo, calere, calui, be warm

19 **sole: sol, solis,** *m.,* sun
   mutamus: muto, mutare, mutavi, mutatum, exchange (in place of our own
      country)
   quis: quis-quid, *inter. adj.,* which, what; **exsul: exsul, exsulis,** *m.,* expatriate

20 **fugit: fugio, fugere, fugi, fugiturum,** flee from, succeed in escaping from

21 **scandit: scando, scandere, scandi, scansum,** board, climb
   aeratas: aeratus, -a, -um, *adj.,* bronze plated, with bronze plated prows
   vitiosa: vitiosus, -a, -um, *adj.,* corrupt, bad

22 **Cura: cura, curae,** *f.,* anxiety (the personified subject of *scandit* and *relinquit)*
    turmas: turma, turmae, *f.,* troop, squadron
    equitum: eques, equitis, *m.,* cavalryman

23 **ocior: ocior-ocius,** *adj.,* swifter
    cervis: cerva, cervae, *f.,* deer
    nimbos: nimbus, nimbi, *m.,* dark cloud, rain cloud, storm cloud

24 **Euro: Eurus, Euri,** *m.,* Eurus, the east wind

25 **laetus: laetus, -a, -um,** *adj.,* happy, joyful
    praesens: praesens, praesentis, *adj.,* present (supply *tempus)*
    animus: animus, animi, *m.,* spirit, mind
    ultra: ultra, *adv.,* beyond

26 **oderit: odi, odisse,** (defective verb) (with an infinitive) disdain (to), be reluctant
       (to); perfect iussive subjuctive
    amara: amarus, -a, -um, *adj.,* bitter, (used substantively) "bitterness"
    lento: lentus, -a, -um, *adj.,* gentle, patient; note the contraposition of *amara* and
       lento.

27 **temperet: tempero, temperare, temperavi, temperatum,** temper (perfect iussive
       subjunctive)
    risu: risus, risus, *m.,* smile

28 **ab omni parte:** a phrase which means "in every respect" or "altogether."
    beatum: beatus, -a, -um, *adj.,* happy, blessed

29 **abstulit: aufero, auferre, abstuli, ablatum,** carry off
    cita: citus, -a, -um, *adj.,* early, untimely; (usually) quick (*Odes* I.37.18)
    mors: mors, mortis, *f.,* death
    Achillem: Achilles, Achillis, *m.,* the great hero Achilles who was killed by Priam's
       son, Paris, when the latter mortally wounded the hero in his heel.

30 **Tithonum: Tithonus, Tithoni,** *m.,* Tithonus, husband of Aurora; Tithonus was
       immortal but also aged forever, not being granted perpetual youth.
    minuit: minuo, minuere, minui, minutum, shrivel (a human being)
    senectus: senectus, senectutis, *f.,* old age

31 **forsan: forsan,** *adv.,* perhaps
    negarit = negaverit

32 **porriget: porrigo, porrigere, porrexi, porrectum,** offer
    hora: hora, horae, *f.,* hour, time, the passing hour

Cura nec turmas equitum relinquit,
ocior cervis et agente nimbos
    ocior Euro.
laetus in praesens animus quod ultra est   25
oderit curare et amara lento
temperet risu; nihil est ab omni
    parte beatum.
abstulit clarum cita mors Achillem,
longa Tithonum minuit senectus,   30
et mihi forsan, tibi quod negarit,
    porriget hora.
te greges centum Siculaeque circum
mugiunt vaccae, tibi tollit hinnitum
apta quadrigis equa, te bis Afro   35
    murice tinctae
vestiunt lanae: mihi parva rura et
spiritum Graiae tenuem Camenae

33   **te:** object of the preposition *circum*; **greges:** grex, gregis, *m.*, herd
    Siculaeque: Siculus, -a, -um, *adj.*, Sicilian

34   **mugiunt:** mugio, mugire, mugivi, mugitum, bellow
    vaccae: vacca, vaccae, *f.*, cow
    tollit: tollo, tollere, sustuli, sublatum, raise
    hinnitum: hinnitus, hinnitus, *m.*, whinny; (with tollit) "whinnies"

35   **apta:** aptus, -a, -um, *adj.*, fit for (with dative)
    quadrigis: quadrigae, quadrigarum, *f. pl.*, chariot; **equa:** equa, equae, *f.*, mare
    Afro: Afer-Afra-Afrum, *adj.*, African; murex was found on the African coast.

36   **murice:** murex, muricis, *m.*, purple dye
    tinctae: tinguo, tinguere, tinxi, tinctus, dye
    bis...tinctae: to produce the true Tyrian dye, renowned in antiquity, the woolwas
      dipped into two different baths, obtained from two different shells.

37   **vestiunt:** vestio, vestire, vestivi, vestitum, clothe
    lanae: lana, lanae, *f.*, wool; (figuratively) clothing
    rura: rus, ruris, *n.*, fields, country estate

38   **spiritum:** spiritus, spiritus, *m.*, breath, inspiration
    Graiae: Graius, -a, -um, *adj.*, Greek; **tenuem:** tenuis-tenue, *adj.*, slight
    Camenae: Camena, Camenae, *f.*, Muse, the native goddess of Roman poetry;
      (figuratively) song

Parca non mendax dedit et malignum
spernere vulgus.   40

39 **Parca: Parca, Parcae,** *f.,* Fate, goddess of fate
mendax: mendax, mendacis, *adj.,* deceiving, deceptive
non mendax = ever truthful
malignum: malignus, -a, -um, *adj.,* malicious, envious

40 **spernere: sperno, spernere, sprevi, spretum,** scorn; the infinitive phrase is the
third object of the verb *dedit;* perhaps best translated "the ability to scorn ..."
vulgus: vulgus, vulgi, *n.,* crowd

Views of two panels from the Ara Pacis Augustae (13 - 9 B.C.). The upper panel, from the west side of the monument, according to most scholars, depicts Aeneas in the act of sacrificing upon his arrival on Italian soil. The small temple in the upper left hand corner, the attendants *(camilli),* the sacrificial animal, and the figure of Aeneas with his head covered give visual testimony to the religious renewal associated with Augustus. The lower panel is believed to portray the mother earth goddess, Tellus, as happy and fertile, surrounded by symbols of nature such as crops, winds, the sea, animals, and, of course, her progeny held in her arms. These represent the prosperity and peace brought to the world by the first Roman emperor.

Odes III.1

1   **profanum: profanus, -a, -um,** *adj.,* before the temple, not sacred, common; unlike people today, who go inside a church to pray, the Romans stood in front of the temple and only the priest entered. Strictly the word refers to those who do not belong in the temple, but figuratively it refers to those who do not understand poetry, namely, the *profani.*
vulgus = volgus: volgus, volgi, *n.,* masses, multitude, crowd
arceo: arceo, arcere, arcui, hold off, keep at a distance, keep away

2   **favete: faveo, favere, favi, fauturus, -a, -um,** be favorable to, (with *linguis)* to abstain from ill-omened speech, keep still, be silent; it was customary for the priest before commencing a rite to ask people to observe silence, since the speaking of words of ill-omen would nullify the effect of the rite.

4   **canto: canto, cantare, cantavi, cantatum,** recite, sing

5   **greges: grex, gregis,** *m.,* flock, (used somewhat contemptuously here) "subjects"; proper word order would be: *(imperium) regum timendorum (est) in proprios greges; imperium Iovis est in reges ipsos;*

6   **imperium: imperium, imperii,** *n.,* rule, sway (power over life and death)
est = extends over

7   **Giganteo: Giganteus, -a, -um,** *adj.,* of the giants; a reference to the battle between Zeus and the giants, the gigantomachy, by which Zeus secured his power; ablative of cause explaining why *clari* (modifying *Iovis)* is appropriate.

8   **cuncta: cunctus, -a, -um,** *adj.,* whole, entire, (used substantively) all things, the world (object of the participle *moventis)*
supercilio: supercilium, supercili(i), *n.,* eyebrow (ablative of means); "by a nod of his brow"
moventis: genitive singular of the present participle of *moveo,* (in this context) shaking

9   **est ut** = it is true that
ordinet: ordino, ordinare, ordinavi, ordinatum, arrange

10 **arbusta: arbustum, arbusti,** *n.,* orchard, tree; *arbustum* is the technical term for a tree or row of trees on which vines were trained
sulcis: sulcus, sulci, *m.,* a furrow
generosior: *comp. adj.* from *generosus, -a, -um, adj.,* of high birth

11 **descendat: descendo, descendere, descendi, descensum,** descend; the wealthy lived on the hills

The first six poems of Book III form a poetic unit traditionally called the Roman Odes. These poems are devoted to the praise of certain attributes deemed essential to the new Rome envisioned by Augustus. Their length sets them apart; their meter is Alcaic; their structure complex. The first four lines of this ode serve as a general introduction for all of the Roman Odes. They alert the reader that these pronouncements will be unique; there is a command to observe a religious silence as though the reader were passing into sacred space, and Horace identifies himself as *sacerdos*. The six Roman Odes address the value of simplicity or frugality (III.1), steadfastness and loyalty (III.2), perseverence and justice (III.3), wisdom and organization (III.4), military courage (III.5), and religious purity (III.6).

Odi profanum vulgus et arceo;
favete linguis: carmina non prius
   audita Musarum sacerdos
   virginibus puerisque canto.
regum timendorum in proprios greges,   5
   reges in ipsos imperium est Iovis,
     clari Giganteo triumpho,
     cuncta supercilio moventis.
est ut viro vir latius ordinet
arbusta sulcis, hic generosior   10
   descendat in Campum petitor,
     moribus hic meliorque fama
contendat, illi turba clientium
sit maior: aequa lege Necessitas

11 **Campum:** this refers to the Campus Martius, a section of Rome near the Tiber
    river which was used (as in this context) for sports, military exercises, and
    elections.
   petitor: petitor, petitoris, *m.,* candidate

12 **moribus: mos, moris,** *m.,* humor, manner; (in plural) morals, character

13 **contendat: contendo, contendere, contendi, contentum,** compete
   illi is a dative of possession.
   turba clientium, the crowd of clients, symbolic of the importance of a man. It was
    a status symbol, like being driven to work in a limousine.

14 **Necessitas: necessitas, necessitatis,** *f.,* fate, destiny, law of nature

15 **sortitur: sortior, sortiri, sortitus sum,** assign by lot, decide the fate of

16 **capax: capax, capacis,** *adj.,* spacious; the urn is *capax* because it holds the lots of all mankind.

17 **destrictus: destringo, destringere, destrinxi, destrictum,** unsheathe; the reference is to the sword of Damocles, who was a flatterer of the Sicilian king Dionysius the Elder. Damocles declared that Dionysius was the most fortunate and wealthy ruler on earth. In reaction, the king invited Damocles to sit on his throne to survey all the wealth which was under his command, as well as to experience the sincere good wishes expressed to the ruler by so many of the ruled. When Damocles took Dionysius' position and surveyed all before him, he noticed that a sword had been suspended over his head by a horsehair. Recognizing the peril of the tyrant's position, he begged Dionysius to restore him to his former obscurity.

   cui = ei cui: the proper word order would be *ei, cui destrictus ensis super impia cervice pendet* ; "for him over whose neck;" the Latin uses a dative particularly with parts of the body where English would use the posessive case.

   impia: with the sense of "guilty" modifies *cervice* but in sense goes with the understood *ei.*

18 **Siculae: Siculus, -a, -um,** *adj.,* of or belonging to Sicily
   dapes: daps, dapis, *f.,* meal, feast

19 **dulcem** = pleasant
   elaborabunt: elaboro, elaborare, elaboravi, elaboratum, develop, produce
   saporem: sapor, saporis, *m.,* taste, sense of taste; here "a keen appetite"

20 **avium: avis, avis,** *f.,* bird
   citharae: cithara, citharae, *f.,* lyre
   cantus: cantus, cantus, m. song; the proper word order is: *cantus avium citharaeque non reducent somnum.*

21 **agrestium: agrestis-agreste,** *adj.,* rustic, wild; "of country-folk"; proper word order would be: *somnus lenis non fastidit humilis domos agrestium virorum umbrosamque ripam; non (fastidit) Tempe agitata Zephyris.*

23 **fastidit: fastidio, fastidire, fastidivi, fastiditum,** feel disgust for, shrink from, despise, shun
   umbrosam: umbrosus, -a, -um, *adj.,* shadowy, shady

3rd sg
pres act ind → sortitur <u>insignis</u> *acc do* et imos;   15
      omne capax movet urna nomen.
destrictus ensis cui super impia
cervice pendet, non Siculae dapes
      dulcem elaborabunt saporem,
        non avium citharaeque cantus   20
somnum reducent: somnus agrestium
lenis virorum non humilis <u>domos</u> *acc do*
      fastidit umbrosamque <u>ripam</u>, *acc do*
        non Zephyris agitata Tempe. *acc do*
p.a.p. desiderantem <u>quod</u> satis est neque *nom subj*   25
tumultuosum sollicitat mare
      nec saevus Arcturi cadentis
        impetus aut orientis Haedi,
non verberatae grandine vineae
fundusque mendax, arbore nunc <u>aquas</u> *acc do* 30

24 **Zephyris: Zephyrus, Zephyri,** *m.,* west wind
    Tempe: Tempe, a neuter plural form which is found only in the nominative,
        accusative or vocative cases; a valley near Mount Olympus in Thessaly noted
        for its beauty; any beautiful valley

26 **tumultuosum: tumultuosus, -a, -um,** *adj.,* full of uproar, noisy, stormy
    sollicitat: sollicito, sollicitare, sollicitavi, sollicitatum, disturb, upset; the subjects
        of this verb include *mare, impetus, vineae* and *fundus.*

27 **saevus: saevus, -a, -um,** *adj.,* cruel, savage
    Arcturi: Arcturus, Arcturi, *m.,* Arcturus, the brightest star of Bootes. The
        constellation rising before the Great Bear, signifying the end of October

28 **impetus: impetus, impetus,** *m.,* onset
    orientis: orior, oriri, ortus sum, arise, rise, stir, get up
    Haedi: Haedus, Haedi, *m.,* Haedi, star(s) in the hand of the celestial formation
        known as the wagoneer *(Auriga),* signifying early October

29 **verberatae: verbero, verberare, verberavi, verberatum,** batter, beat
    grandine: grando, grandinis, *f.,* hail; **vineae: vinea, vineae,** *f.,* vineyard

30 **fundus: fundus, fundi,** *m.,* farm, estate; *fundus* and *arbor* are personified.
    mendax: mendax, mendacis, *adj.,* false, mendacious, deceptive; since the farm did
        not produce the crops it promised, here the word means "unproductive."

31 **culpante: culpo, culpare, culpavi, culpatum,** blame, find fault with; the ablative
    absolute *(arbore culpante)* gives justification for the epithet *mendax* that was
    applied to the personified *fundus.*
    torrentia: torreo, torrere, torrui, tostum, dry up, scorch

32 **iniquas: iniquus, -a, -um,** *adj.,* unfair, harsh

33 **contracta: contraho, contrahere, contraxi, contractum,** contract
    pisces: piscis, piscis, *m.,* fish

34 **iactis: iacio, iacere, ieci, iactum,** (with *fundamenta*) lay foundations; the technical
    term for putting in the foundation for a massive building, similar to our phrase
    "to sink a foundation."
    molibus: moles, molis, *f.,* mass (of stone), structure (equivalent to *fundamenta*);
    the point here is that palatial residences were built over the water, as at the town
    of Baiae, a seaside resort on the bay of Naples. The expression is an obvious
    hyperbole.
    huc = in altum
    frequens: frequens, frequentis, *adj.,* crowded, densely packed; take *cum famulis*
    (line 36) with *frequens.*

35 **caementa: caementum, caementi,** *n.,* rubble, cement, foundation
    demittit: demitto, demittere, demisi, demissum, drop, let down
    redemptor: redemptor, -oris, *m.,* contractor; "the contractor with his throngs of
    workers"

36 **famulis: famulus, famuli,** *m.,* servant, slave, worker
    dominus: dominus, domini, *m.,* master, owner

37 **fastidiosus: fastidiosus, -a, -um,** *adj.,* (with genitive) scornful of, sick and tired of,
    disdainful of
    Timor: Timor, Timoris, *m.,* Fear (a personification)
    Minae: Minae, Minarum, *f. pl.,* Threat(s) (a personification)

38 **eodem: eodem,** *adv.,* to the same place
    quo: quo, *adv.,* (indicating direction) where, to where

39 **decedit: decedo, decedere, decessi, decessum,** withdraw, get off, disembark
    aerata: aeratus, -a, -um, *adj.,* bronze-prowed
    triremi: triremis-trireme, *adj.,* used substantively as a feminine noun to denote
    a ship with three banks of oars on each side, a trireme, huge yacht; yachts and
    horses imply not only speed but also the status symbols of the very rich.

40 **post: post,** *prep.,* behind; **equitem: eques, equitis,** *m.,* horseman, rider
    Cura: Cura, Curae, *f.,* Anxiety (a personification)

culpante, nunc torrentia agros
sidera, nunc hiemes iniquas.
contracta pisces aequora sentiunt
iactis in altum molibus; huc frequens
caementa demittit redemptor   35
cum famulis dominusque terrae
fastidiosus: sed Timor et Minae
scandunt eodem quo dominus, neque
decedit aerata triremi et
post equitem sedet atra Cura.   40
quodsi dolentem nec Phrygius lapis
nec purpurarum sidere clarior
delenit usus nec Falerna
vitis Achaemeniumque costum,
cur invidendis postibus et novo   45

41 **quodsi: quodsi,** *conj.,* but if
dolentem: doleo, dolere, dolui, dolitum, grieve, be in distress; (used substantively)
   "one in distress"
Phrygius: Phrygius, -a, -um, *adj.,* Phrygian, Trojan, in the northwest areas of
   Asia Minor; here intended to suggest that the remoteness of the stone quarry
   contributes to its supposed value.
lapis: lapis, lapidis, *m.,* marble (quarried in Phrygia and valued for its various
   hues)

42 **purpurarum: purpura, purpurae,** *f.,* purple garment, splendid clothing
sidere: sidus, sideris, *n.,* star

43 **delenit: delenio, delenire, delenivi, delenitum,** soothe, calm down
usus: usus, usus, *m.,* use of, wearing of
Falerna: Falernus, -a, -um, *adj.,* Falernian, of or belonging to a district in the
   northern part of Campania, a costly wine

44 **vitis: vitis, vitis,** *f.,* vine, vine branch; (figuratively) wine
Achaemenium: Achaemenius, -a, -um, *adj.,* Persian
costum: costum, costi, *n.,* perfume

45 **postibus: postis, postis** *m.,* doorpost; (figuratively) door
novo: novus, -a, -um, *adj.,* modern

sublime ritu moliar atrium?   *abl/manner*
    cur valle permutem Sabina
        divitias operosiores?

aco do

46 **sublime: sublimis-sublime,** *adj.,* lofty, towering high
   ritu: ritus, ritus, *m.,* rite, style, fashion
   moliar: molior, moliri, molitus sum, do with great effort, struggle to build

47 **valle: vallis, vallis,** *f.,* valley; hyperbolic metonymy to suggest where Horace's
        simple Sabine farm was located.
   permutem: permuto, permutare, permutavi, permutatum, change completely
   Sabina: Sabinus, -a, -um, *adj.,* of or belonging to Sabine country

48 **operosiores:** *comp. adj.* from *operosus, -a, -um, adj.,* troublesome

Odes III.2

The second Roman Ode begins with the praise of frugality or simplicity sounded in the previous poem. Horace gives us a rather romantic picture of the bravery and courage on foreign battlefields that the young Roman warrior should show. The innocence and preparedness of a young man for battle must be informed by the understanding that death does not respect age or inexperience. The second half of the poem, introduced by *virtus,* takes up the political or domestic virtues. The public figure is not to be swayed by popular will, trades earthly things for those above, and knows how to keep a proper silence. Courage and loyalty have their own reward. The meter is Alcaic as in *Odes* I.9.

Angustam amice pauperiem pati
robustus acri militia puer
    condiscat et Parthos feroces
        vexet eques metuendus hasta
vitamque sub divo et trepidis agat   5

1   **angustam: angustus, -a, -um,** *adj.,* harsh, pinching
     amice: amice, *adv.,* gladly, with good will
     pauperiem: pauperies, pauperiei, *f.,* poverty
     pati: patior, pati, passus sum, suffer

2   **robustus: robustus, -a, -um,** *adj.,* hardened (by)
     militia: militia, militiae, *f.,* military service (ablative of cause with *robustus*)
     puer: the military age was seventeen

3   **condiscat: condisco, condiscere, condidici,** learn thoroughly
     Parthos: Parthi, Parthorum, *m. pl.,* the Parthians, a people in central Asia Minor
        to whom Crassus lost the Roman standards *(signa)* in the battle at Carrhae in
        53 B.C.

4   **vexet: vexo, vexare, vexavi, vexatum,** harass
     eques: in apposition with the subject of *vexet,* "as a cavalryman"; since the Parthians'
        main strength was in the cavalry, Horace encourages his friend to excel in the
        same branch of service.
     hasta: hasta, hastae, *f.,* spear (ablative of cause)

5   **divo: divum, divi,** *n.,* the sky, open air
     trepidis: trepidus, -a, -um, *adj.,* hazardous, stirring
     agat: ago, agere, egi, actum, (with *vita*) spend (life)

6   **illum** = (object of *prospiciens)* him (i.e., such a young man as has just been described)
    hosticis: hosticus, -a, -um, *adj.,* hostile

7   **matrona: matrona, matronae,** *f.,* wife, consort
    tyranni = **regis**

8   **prospiciens: prospicio, prospicere, prospexi, prospectum,** look into the distance at, have a view, look out at
    adulta: adultus, -a, -um, *adj.,* mature, grown up; this scene alludes to the Homeric τειχοσκοπια, the view from the walls; *matrona* may suggest Amata and *adulta virgo* Lavinia, serving to lend epic proportions to the scene.

9   **suspiret: suspiro, suspirare, suspiravi, suspiratum,** sigh (introducing the thought, "Ah, let not …" Although both *matrona* and *virgo* are the subjects of the verb *suspiret,* the whole clause from *"eheu ... caedes"* expresses the feelings only of the girl.
    eheu: eheu, *interj.,* what, Ah!
    rudis: rudis-rude, *adj.,* (with genitive) untrained in, unskilled in
    agminum: agmen, agminis, *n.,* marching column; (in the plural) warfare

10 **sponsus: sponsus, sponsi,** *m.,* (her) fiancé
    lacessat: laceso, lacessere, lacessivi, lacessitum, provoke
    regius: regius, -a, -um, *adj.,* royal, of royal blood
    asperum: asper-aspera-asperum, *adj.,* rough; dangerous

11 **tactu: tactus, tactus,** *m.,* touch; **quem:** this refers to the soldier, not the lion
    cruenta: cruentus, -a, -um, *adj.,* bloody; (with *ira* in line 12) "rage for blood"

12 **rapit: rapio, rapere, rapui, raptum,** sweeps along, causes to rush
    caedes: caedes, caedis, *f.,* carnage, slaughter

13 **decorum: decorus, -a, -um,** *adj.,* glorious, noble, that which confers *decus* (honor or glory)

14 **fugacem: fugax, fugacis,** *adj.,* fleeing

15 **parcit: parco, parcere, peperci, parsum,** spare (with the dative)
    imbellis: imbellis-imbelle, *adj.,* unfit for war, unwarlike, peaceful
    iuventae: iuventa, iuventae, *f.,* youth

16 **poplitibus: poples, poplitis,** *m.,* hollow of the knee, knee
    tergo: tergum, tergi, *n.,* back; being wounded in the back and in the hollow of the knee prove the man a coward.

in rebus. illum ex moenibus hosticis
    matrona bellantis tyranni
        prospiciens et adulta virgo
suspiret, eheu, ne rudis agminum
sponsus lacessat regius asperum   10
    tactu leonem, quem cruenta
        per medias rapit ira caedes.
dulce et decorum est pro patria mori:
mors et fugacem persequitur virum,
    nec parcit imbellis iuventae   15
        poplitibus timidove tergo.
Virtus repulsae nescia sordidae
intaminatis fulget honoribus,
    nec sumit aut ponit securis
        arbitrio popularis aurae.   20
Virtus, recludens immeritis mori

17   **Virtus: Virtus, Virtutis,** *f.,* personification of courage
    repulsae: repulsa, repulsae, *f.,* defeat; this is the technical term for defeat at the
        polls and its use signals the shift from the military to the political arena. This
        is reinforced by the words *honoribus,* here having the denotation of honor and
        the connotation of high office as in *Odes* I.1.8.
    nescia: nescius, -a, -um, *adj.,* ignorant of, unfamiliar with
    sordidae: sordidus, -a, -um, *adj.,* foul, unclean, disgraceful (the emphasis is on
        sordida)

18   **intaminatis: intaminatus, -a, -um,** *adj.,* uncontaminated, undefiled
    fulget: fulgeo, fulgere, fulsi, shine, glitter, be conspicuous, be illustrious

19   **ponit = deponit**
    securis: securis, securis, *m., f.,* ax, the fasces, a bundle of rods and an ax tied together,
        carried by lictors preceding men holding high office such as quaestors, consuls,
        praetors, dictators. Even the emperor had lictors in virtue of the magistracy that
        he assumed. This is an immediate symbol of the power over life and death.

20   **arbitrio: arbitrium, arbitri(i),** *n.,* control, will, decision
    popularis: popularis-populare, *adj.,* favoring the people, the people's
    aurae: aura, aurae, *f.,* breeze; symbolic of the quickly changing public opinion

21   **recludens: recludo, recludere, reclusi, reclusum,** open, disclose
    immeritis: immeritus, -a, -um, *adj.,* undeserving (used substantively)
    mori: morior, mori, mortuus sum, die

22 **caelum: caelum, caeli,** *n.,* heaven, the gates of heaven
negata: modifies *via*, an ablative of means; "along a path denied (to others)"
iter: iter, itineris, *n.,* route, journey

23 **coetus: coetus, coetus,** *m.,* crowd
vulgaris: vulgaris-vulgare, *adj.,* common
udam: udus, -a, -um, *adj.,* moist, damp, humid

24 **humum: humus, humi,** *f.,* ground; *udam humum* is a metaphor for the grave as
well as for the ambitions and lowly pursuits of the common man.
penna: penna, pennae, *f.,* feather, wing

25 **et: et,** *adv.,* also
tuta: tutus, -a, -um, *adj.,* sure

26 **merces: merces, mercedis,** *f.,* wages, reward; Horace makes a clever allusion to
one of Augustus' favorite maxims, *"Est mercedes fideli silentio."*
vetabo: veto, vetare, vetavi or **vetui, vetitum,** forbid
Cereris: Ceres, Cereris, *f.,* Ceres (the Greek Demeter), the goddess of grain
sacrum: sacrum, sacri, *n.,* sacred rite

27 **vulgarit = vulgaverit: vulgo, vulgare, vulgavi, vulgatum,** divulge
arcanae: arcanus, -a, -um, *adj.,* secret; modifies *Cereris* but goes in sense with
sacrum; the secret rite(s) of Ceres; the initiates (among whom was Augustus)
were never allowed to divulge the secrets of the Eleusinian mysteries. No one
ever did and so even today we don't know what they were.

28 **sit:** dependent upon *vetabo*
trabibus: trabs or **trabes, trabis,** *f.,* rafter, (figuratively) roof
fragilemque: fragilis-fragile, *adj.,* fragile, frail

29 **solvat: solvo, solvere, solvi, solutum,** unfasten (to set sail)
phaselon: phaselus, phaseli, *m.,* skiff, boat; the Greek accusative of this word is
phaselon.
Diespiter: Diespiter, Diespitris, *m.,* Jupiter; this word from early Roman worship
lends a sense of inevitability to the poem's close.

30 **neglectus: neglectus, -a, -um,** *adj.,* outraged, neglected, slighted
incesto: incestus, -a, -um, *adj.,* unclean, impure, guilty
addidit: addo, addere, addidi, additum, add to
integrum: integer-integra-integrum, *adj.,* whole, pure, innocent

caelum, negata temptat iter via,
  coetusque vulgaris et udam
    spernit humum fugiente penna.
est et fideli tuta silentio   25
merces: vetabo, qui Cereris sacrum
  vulgarit arcanae, sub isdem
    sit trabibus fragilemque mecum
solvat phaselon: saepe Diespiter
neglectus incesto addidit integrum   30
  raro antecedentem scelestum
    deseruit pede Poena claudo.

31 **raro: raro,** *adv.,* rarely
   antecedentem: antecedo, antecedere, antecessi, precede; here with adversative
      force, "even though getting a head start"
   scelestum: scelestus, -a, -um, *adj.,* wicked, criminal (used substantively); it is
      Jupiter's tendency to involve the innocent with the wicked that makes the speaker
      of the poem refuse to live under the same roof or sail with a man who dared to
      commit the sacrilege of divulging the secret rites of Demeter.

32 **deseruit: desero, deserere, deserui, desertum,** abandon (the chase of), forsake,
      failed to catch up to
   Poena: Poena, Poenae, *f.,* Vengeance, Retribution, goddess of punishment
   claudo: claudus, -a, -um, *adj.,* limping, halting, lame

Odes III.9

1   **donec: donec,** *conj.,* as long as; **gratus: gratus, -a, -um,** *adj.,* pleasing, attractive

2   **quisquam: quisquam, cuiusquam,** *pron.,* anyone, anybody; used adjectively for
     ullus and taken with *iuvenis*
     potior: potior-potius, *adj.,* rather/more preferable, better, superior, more favored
     bracchia: bracchium, bracchi(i), *n.,* arm; **candidae: candidus, -a, -um,** *adj.,*
     white

3   **cervici: cervix, cervicis,** *f.,* neck; **dabat = circumdabat** = put (his arm) around
     (with dative)

4   **Persarum: Persae, Persarum,** *m. pl.,* the Persians, used with *rege* to represent vast
     wealth; **vigui: vigeo, vigere, vigui,** thrive, flourish
     beatior: beatus, -a, -um, *adj.,* happy

5   **alia: alius, -a, -ud,** *adj.,* other, another; used as a substantive in the ablative case
     magis: magis, *adv.,* more

6   **arsisti: ardeo, ardere, arsi,** burn with passion; this word rachets up the speaker's
     emotion beyond that implied by *gratus eram* (line 1). Lydia is one of Horace's
     amicae; the others include Pyrrha (I.5), Lalage (I.22) and Chloe (I.23).

7   **multi = magni**
     nominis: nomen, nominis, *n.,* reputation, fame (genitive expressing quality)

8   **clarior: clarus, -a, -um,** *adj.,* famous, well known
     Ilia: Ilia, Iliae, *f.,* poetic name for Rhea Silvia, daughter of Numitor and mother of
     Romulus and Remus; *Ilia* is an ablative of comparison.

9   **Me** contrasts sharply with the first person of the previous line.
     Thraessa: Thraessus, -a, -um, *adj.,* a Thracian
     Chloe: Chloe, Chloes, *f.,* Chloe, a Greek female name

10 **dulcis: dulcis-dulce,** *adj.,* sweet; **docta: doctus, -a, -um,** *adj.,* versed in, learned
     modos: modus, modi, *m.,* meter; poetry (accusative of respect with *docta*)
     citharae: cithara, citharae, *f.,* lyre; *sciens* governs the genitive case here.
     sciens: scio, scire, scivi, scitum, know, understand, know how to use

11 **metuam: metuo, metuere, metui,** fear, be afraid of
     mori: morior, mori, mortuus sum, die

12 **parcent: parco, parcere, peperci, parsum,** spare (with dative)
     animae: anima, animae, *f.,* spirit, life, "darling"; a phrase from Plautus
     captures the spirit of these ideas: *anima est amica amanti; si abest,*
     nullus est: a lover's girl is his life; if she is away he is no one.

This playful little dialogue (a sort of lovers' duel) involves the quarrel and reconciliation of Lydia and her unnamed lover. The speakers try to outdo one another in the subtle pairings of their quatrains. Compare the one-upsmanship of Acme and Septimius in Catullus 45. The meter is second Asclepiadean as seen in *Odes* I.3.

Donec gratus eram tibi
nec quisquam potior bracchia candidae
   cervici iuvenis dabat,
Persarum vigui rege beatior.
    'donec non alia magis   5
arsisti neque erat Lydia post Chloen,
   multi Lydia nominis
Romana vigui clarior Ilia.'
    me nunc Thraessa Chloe regit,
dulcis docta modos et citharae sciens,   10
   pro qua non metuam mori,
si parcent animae fata superstiti.
    'me torret face mutua
Thurini Calais filius Ornyti,
   pro quo bis patiar mori,   15
si parcent puero fata superstiti.'
    quid si prisca redit Venus

12 **superstiti: superstes, superstitis,** *adj.,* surviving, outliving, remain alive after another's death; "spare my darling and let her live"

13 **torret: torreo, torrere, torrui, tostum,** burn, scorch; this corresponds to *arsisti* of line 6.
   face: fax, facis, *f.,* torch; (figuratively) flame, passion

14 **Thurini: Thurinus, -a, -um,** *adj.,* belonging to Thurii, a city of Lucania, on the gulf of Tarentum, near the site of Sybaris; these references counterpoint the associations of *Thraessa* (line 9).
   Calais is the name of Lydia's new boyfriend.
   Ornyti: Ornytus, Ornyti, *m.,* Ornytus, father of Calais

15 **patiar: patior, pati, passus sum,** suffer, permit, allow, be willing to

17 **prisca: priscus, -a, -um,** *adj.,* orginal, pure, first
   Venus: used figuratively for love

diductosque iugo cogit aeneo, *nom subj*
    si flava excutitur Chloe
reiectaeque patet ianua Lydiae?   20
    'quamquam sidere pulchrior *abl comparison*
ille est, tu levior cortice et improbo *abl comparison*
    iracundior Hadria,
tecum vivere amem, tecum obeam libens. *nom adj*

18 **diductos: diduco, diducere, diduxi, diductum,** draw apart, separate; (used substantively) "those now separated"
  iugo: iugum, iugi, *n.,* yoke
  cogit: cogo = co+ago, bring together; this is the opposite of *deduco = diduco.*
  aeneo: aeneus, -a, -um, *adj.,* bronze; *iugo aeneo* is an ablative of means with *cogit* and signifies (figuratively) an indissoluable bond

19 **flava: flavus, -a, -um,** *adj.,* yellow, blond, reddish-yellow, golden
  excutitur: excutio, excutere, excussi, excussum, cast aside, jilt

20 **reiectaeque: reicio, reicere, reieci, reiectum,** reject
  patet: pateo, patere, patui, stand open, lie open; *Lydiae* is dative case; *ianua* is used metaphorically to symbolize Lydia's openness to Horace.

21 **quamquam: quamquam,** *conj.,* although; this governs *est* in line 22 and *es* which is understood in lines 22-23.
  pulchrior: the Romans applied *pulcher* equally to both sexes where we would use "beautiful" for females and "handsome" for males.

22 **levior:** a *comp. adj.* derived from *levis-leve, adj.,* light, (figuratively) buoyant; the point seems to be the ease with which change is made, so "fickle" seems appropriate; yet with *cortice,* perhaps "more buoyant than cork"
  cortice: cortex, corticis, *m./f.,* cork
  improbo: improbus, -a, -um, *adj.,* restless, violent, unruly; *improbus* generally signifies "that which exceeds normal limits" and therefore must be translated according to the meaning of the noun it modifies.

23 **iracundior:** a *comp. adj.* from *iracundus, -a, -um, adj.,* easily provoked, irritable, angry; **Hadria: Hadria, Hadriae,** *m.,* the Adriatic Sea, the sea between Italy's east coast and modern Yugoslavia and Greece; *Hadria* is an ablative of comparison.

24 **obeam: obeo, obire, obivi (obii), obitum,** die; sometimes *mortem* appears with this verb and the sense is then "to meet one's death".
  libens: libens, libentis, *adj.,* willing, ready, glad; used here with adverbial force

A view of the structural remains of a Roman villa, thought to be Horace's Sabine farm, near the town of Tivoli. This villa or farm was given to the poet by Augustus through the patronage of Maecenas. Many feel that the spring addressed in III.13 was orginally a part of this villa. It is not absolutely certain that this site belonged to Horace, but circumstances and associations seem compelling.

Odes III.13

1   **fons: fons, fontis,** *m.,* fountain, spring; **Bandusiae: Bandusia, Bandusiae,** *f.,* a pleasant spring near Venusia, the birthplace of Horace
splendidior: splendidus, -a, -um, *adj.,* sparkling, glittering, brilliant
vitro: vitrum, vitri, *n.,* glass

2   **digne: dignus, -a, -um,** *adj.,* worthy (with ablative)

3   **cras: cras,** *adv.,* tomorrow; **haedo: haedus, haedi,** *m.,* a young goat, kid
donaberis: dono, donare, donavi, donatum, honor by a gift, offer, give

4   **cui:** a dative of reference equivalent to a possessive genitive; "whose brow"
frons: frons, frontis, *f.,* brow; **turgida: turgidus, -a, -um,** *adj.,* swollen
cornibus: cornu, cornus, *n.,* horn

5   **Venerem** and **proelia** are metonymy for love and war respectively; the *proelia* will be battles with his rivals because of love.
destinat: destino, destinare, destinavi, destinatum, be destined, be marked out for, foretaken

6   **gelidos: gelidus, -a, -um,** *adj.,* chilly, cold
inficiet: inficio, inficere, infeci, infectum, stain, tint

7   **rubro: ruber-rubra-rubrum,** *adj.,* red; **rivos: rivus, rivi,** *m.,* stream, brook

8   **lascivi: lascivus, -a, -um,** *adj.,* playful, frolicsome, frisky
suboles: suboles, subolis, *f.,* offspring; **gregis: grex, gregis,** *m.,* flock

9   **flagrantis: flagrans, flagrantis,** *adj.,* blazing, hot; **atrox: atrox, atrocis,** *adj.,* savage, harsh, fierce; **hora: hora, horae,** *f.,* season
Caniculae: Canicula, Caniculae, *f.,* the Dog Star (Sirius), symbolizing a time of intense summer heat

10   **nescit: nescio, nescire, nescivi, nescitum,** not to know; here in the sense of "be able to"; **frigus: frigus, frigoris,** *n.,* cold
amabile: amabilis-amabile, *adj.,* loving, beloved

11   **fessis: fessus, -a, -um,** *adj.,* weary, weary from; **tauris: taurus, tauri,** *m.,* bull, ox
vomere: vomer, vomeris, *m.,* ploughshare, (figuratively) plow

12   **praebes: praebeo, praebere, praebui, praebitum,** hold out, offer
pecori: pecus, pecoris, *n.,* flock; **vago: vagus, -a, -um,** *adj.,* wandering; in contrast to the oxen which are tied to the plow

13   **fies: fio, fieri, factus sum,** become, prove to be
nobilium: nobilis-nobile, *adj.,* well-known, famous

Horace writes this poem in hymnal form to an unknown fountain which some scholars identify as a spring located on the grounds of a villa outside Tivoli, thought to have belonged to the poet. Horace uses a series of contrasts (the hot red blood of the kid versus the cold clear water of the fountain and the young life cut short by sacrifice versus the permanence of the living spring) to muse on what is permanent and what is transient. Poetry transcends the divine and the human and will therefore lend immortality to its subjects, including this fountain. The meter is fourth Asclepiadean as in *Odes* I.5.

O fons Bandusiae splendidior vitro
dulci digne mero non sine floribus,
   cras donaberis haedo,
     cui frons turgida cornibus
primis et venerem et proelia destinat;   5
frustra: nam gelidos inficiet tibi
   rubro sanguine rivos
     lascivi suboles gregis.
te flagrantis atrox hora Caniculae
nescit tangere, tu frigus amabile   10
   fessis vomere tauris
     praebes et pecori vago.
fies nobilium tu quoque fontium,
me dicente cavis impositam ilicem
   saxis, unde loquaces   15
     lymphae desiliunt tuae.

14 **me...dicente:** an ablative absolute with a causal force, "because I sing a song of the oak tree..."

    cavis: cavus, -a, -um, *adj.,* hollow; the tree shades the source of the stream and by its position creates a hollow; the waters travel down the rocky surface inside this hollow and create by their downward flow the conversation with which the hollow reverberates.

    impositam: impono, imponere, imposui, impositum, place upon, put

    ilicem: ilex, ilicis, *f.,* holm-oak, oak tree (modified by *impositam*)

15 **loquaces: loquax, loquacis,** *adj.,* talkative, speaking, baffling; the spring is personified; here, though "babbling waters"

16 **lymphae: lympha, lymphae,** *f.,* water
    desiliunt: desilio, desilire, desilui, desultum, leap down, jump down

Odes III.30

1 **Exegi: exigo, exigere, exegi, exactum,** build up, finish
monumentum: monumentum, monumenti, *n.,* that which preserves the remembrance of anything, a memorial, a monument; this can be any written record or document or literary work; undoubtedly Horace visualizes his three books of Odes as his *monumentum.*
aere: aes, aeris, *n.,* bronze; perhaps a reference to the displays of statues and public records in Rome such as the twelve tables
perennius: *comp. adv.* from *perennis-perenne, adj.,* lasting, enduring

2 **regalique: regalis-regale,** *adj.,* royal, regal
situ: situs, situs, *m.,* structure
pyramidum: pyramis, pyramidis, *f.,* pyramid
altius: *comp. adv,* from *altus, -a, -um, adj.,* high, lofty, tall

3 **imber: imber, imbris,** *m.,* rain
edax: edax, edacis, *adj.,* destructive, erosive
Aquilo: Aquilo, Aquilonis, *m.,* north wind
impotens: impotens, impotentis, *adj.,* not having power over oneself, furious, uncontrollable

4 **diruere: diruo, diruere, dirui, dirutum,** pull apart, destroy, wreck
innumerabilis: innumerabilis-innumerabile, *adj.,* countless, innumerable

5 **series: series, seriei,** *f.,* series

6 **moriar: morior, mori, mortuus sum,** die

7 **vitabit: vito, vitare, vitavi, vitatum,** avoid
Libitinam: Libitina, Libitinae, *f.,* Libitina, the goddess of corpses, in whose temple everything pertaining to burials was sold or hired out, and where the death registers were kept; (figuratively) death
Usque has the notion of "on and on" and belongs with *crescam.*
postera: posterus, -a, -um, *adj.,* future, of posterity

8 **crescam: cresco, crescere, crevi, cretum,** increase, grow
laude: laus, laudis, *f.,* praise
recens: recens, recentis, *adj.,* fresh
Capitolium: Capitolium, Capitoli(i), *n.,* the Capitoline Hill, the symbol of the supremacy of Rome

9 **scandet: scando, scandere, scandi, scansum,** climb
The reference to the *pontifex* associates the permanence of the poet's completed craft with the unshakable continuity of Roman religious practices; his poetry possesses its own immortality.

This final poem of Book III has been traditionally called the *sphragis* poem, the "seal-ring" poem. A seal placed upon a finished product was used to signify the completeness of the article. As if wrapping the collection, Horace finishes by using the first Asclepiadean meter which he has used only once before, in *Odes* I.1. The poet places his work's enduring qualities beside the visual symbols of Rome's permanence. His achievement of taking Greek songs and adapting them to the Italian language will outlast any other kind of monument.

Exegi monumentum aere perennius
regalique situ pyramidum altius,
quod non imber edax, non Aquilo impotens
possit diruere aut innumerabilis
annorum series et fuga temporum.   5
non omnis moriar, multaque pars mei
vitabit Libitinam: usque ego postera
crescam laude recens, dum Capitolium
scandet cum tacita virgine pontifex.
dicar, qua violens obstrepit Aufidus 10
et qua pauper aquae Daunus agrestium
regnavit populorum, ex humili potens
princeps Aeolium carmen ad Italos

10 **dicar,** in the sense of pronounced, spoken of, "sung"
violens: violens, violentis, *adj.,* violent, wild, raging
obstrepit: obstrepo, obstrepere, obstrepui, obstrepitum, resound, roar
Aufidus: Aufidus, Aufidi, *m.,* a river in Apulia, Horace's birthplace

11 **pauper: pauper, pauperis,** *adj.,* (with genitive) poor (in)
Daunus: Daunus, Dauni, *m.,* Daunus, first king of Apulia, who according to tradition
    was a refugee from Illyricum; like Horace he had a humble beginning
agrestium: agrestis-agreste, *adj.,* rustic

12 **populorum,** genitive with *regnavit*
humili: humilis-humile, *adj.,* humble, lowly; (used substantively) "humble birth"
potens: potens, potentis, *adj.,* powerful, influential; (used substantively) "an
    influential person" or "a ruler"

13 **princeps: princeps, principis,** *m.,* first man, most distinguished; the word brings
    to mind Augustus, who took the title *princeps.*

deduxisse modos. sume superbiam
quaesitam meritis et mihi Delphica _adj meaning_ 15
lauro cinge volens, Melpomene, comam. _2nd sg pres act imp_

adj means

13 **Aeolium: Aeolius, -a, -um,** *adj.,* Aeolian, the dialect of Sappho and Alcaeus; there
   are 88 poems in *Odes* I-III; 22 are in Sapphic and 33 in Alcaic meter.
   Italos: Italus, -a, -um, *adj.,* Italian; this adjective nationalizes the poet's
   achievements.

14 **deduxisse: deduco, deducere, deduxi, deductum,** adapt; governed by *dicar;*
   princeps … deduxisse = "as the first to have adapted …"
   modos: modus, modi, *m.,* measure, meter, (figuratively) poetry
   sume: sumo, sumere, sumpsi, sumptum, take, assume
   superbiam: superbia, superbiae, *f.,* pride, proud honor

15 **quaesitam: quaero, quaerere, quaesivi, quaesitum,** gain, win; here with *meritis,*
   there is the sense of "deserved."
   meritis: meritum, meriti, *n.,* achievement, merit
   mihi: a dative of reference, which, as usual, takes the place of the possessive adjective
   meus, -a, -um
   Delphica: a reference to Apollo of Delphi and the laurel wreath which is sacred to
   him

16 **lauro: laurus, lauri,** *f.,* laurel
   cinge: cingo, cingere, cinxi, cinctum, surround, wreathe
   volens: volo, velle, volui, wish, want, be willing to; used here with adverbial force,
   "willingly" or "graciously"
   Melpomene: the muse of tragedy, here representing poetry in general
   comam: coma, comae, *f.,* hair, (figuratively) head

A representation of the poet Ovid done by Luca Signorelli (1441-1523) as a part of the fresco work of the south transcept chapel in the great cathedral of Orvieto, a town some fifty miles north of Rome. The portrait shows the poet with a wreath of laurel signifying his artistic and prophetic gifts.

Odes IV.7

1   **diffugere = diffugerunt: diffugio, diffugere, diffugi, diffugiturum,** flee in different directions, disappear, melt
    nives: nix, nivis, *f.,* snow; **redeunt: redeo, redire, redii, reditum,** return
    gramina: gramen, graminis, *n.,* grass (subject of *redeunt)*
    campis: campus, campi, *m.,* (untilled) field

2   **arboribus: arbor, arboris,** *f.,* tree
    comae: coma, comae, *f.,* hair, (figuratively) foliage (also subject of *redeunt)*

3   **mutat: muto, mutare, mutavi, mutatum,** change; the earth undergoes change as to its (annual) succession of seasons.
    vices: vicis (genitive singular), *vicem* (accusative singular), *vice* (ablative singular), *f.,* succession; the noun lacks a nominative singular; its plural form means "seasons."
    decrescentia: decresco, decrescere, decrevi, decretum, diminish, subside, recede
    ripas: ripa, ripae, *f.,* bank (of a river)

4   **praetereunt: praetereo, praeterire, praeterii, praeteritum,** go by, flow along, flow within

5   **Gratia: Gratia, Gratiae,** *f.,* a Grace, one of the three Graces
    Nymphis: Nympha, Nymphae, *f.,* nymph
    geminisque: geminus, -a, -um, *adj.,* twin
    sororibus: soror, sororis, *f.,* sister; *geminis sororibus* to be taken with *Gratia*
    audet: audeo, audere, ausus sum, dare, venture

6   **nuda: nudus, -a, -um,** *adj.,* nude; the sudden warmth of spring occasions a passionate dance; because the cold is gone, they can dance naked.
    choros: chorus, chori, *m.,* band of dancers, dancing

7   **immortalia: immortalis-immortale,** *adj.,* deathless, immortal; used substantively, "immortality"
    speres: spero, sperare, speravi, speratum, hope; the substantive clause *ne speres immortalia* is the object of the verb *monet.*
    almum: almus, -a, -um, *adj.,* nourishing, kind, genial

8   **rapit: rapio, rapere, rapui, raptum,** rush on, make (the day) rush by
    hora: hora, horae, *f.,* hour; it makes time move so fast that it robs us of its enjoyment.

9   **frigora: frigus, frigoris,** *n.,* cold
    mitescunt: mitesco, mitescere, grow mild
    Zephyris: Zephyrus, Zephyri, *m.,* west wind; "under the influence of …"
    ver: ver, veris, *n.,* spring
    proterit: protero, protere, protrivi, protritum, tread upon, tread on the heels of
    aestas: aestas, aestatis, *f.,* summer

Horace chronicles the change of seasons and reflects on the cycle of time's passage. The constant renewal of nature's cycles acts as a counterpoise to the finality of human existence. We die. The mythological references function as reminders of those who have tried, but failed, to break the bonds of death. The meter, third Archilochian, offers a full line of dactylic hexameter followed by one half of the dactylic pentameter. The result suggests the elegiac couplet, minus one half of the regular pentameter line. Connections in theme and in meter may be made with Horace's earlier spring poem, *Odes* I.4.

Diffugere nives, redeunt iam gramina campis
    arboribusque comae;
mutat terra vices, et decrescentia ripas
    flumina praetereunt;
Gratia cum Nymphis geminisque sororibus audet
    ducere nuda choros.
immortalia ne speres, monet annus et almum
    quae rapit hora diem:
frigora mitescunt Zephyris, ver proterit aestas
    interitura, simul   10
pomifer Autumnus fruges effuderit, et mox
    bruma recurrit iners.
damna tamen celeres reparant caelestia lunae:

10 **interitura: intereo, interire, interii, interitum,** perish
    simul = simul ac = simula atque, *conj.,* as soon as

11 **pomifer: pomifer-pomifera-pomiferum,** *adj.,* bountiful, fruitful
    Autumnus: autumnus, autumni, *m.,* autumn
    fruges: fruges, frugum, *f. pl.,* crops
    effuderit: effundo, effundere, effudi, effusum, pour forth
    mox: mox, *adv.,* soon; (in a series) then, next

12 **bruma: bruma, brumae,** *f.,* (dead of) winter
    recurrit: recurro, recurrere, recurri, recursum, return
    iners: iners, inertis, *adj.,* lifeless

13 **damna: damnum, damni,** *n.,* loss
    celeres: celer-celeris-celere, *adj.,* swift; swiftly changing
    reparant: reparo, reparare, reparavi, reparatum, repair, restore
    caelestia: caelestis-caeleste, *adj.,* of or pertaining to the sky, heavenly

14 **nos:** this is contrasting to the moons *(lunae)* of line 13 which fall and rise; the plural form suggests "the moon each night" as would *soles* suggest "the sun each day"; *nos* configures all of humanity.
     decidimus: decido, decidere, decidi, fall, descend

15 **quo: quo,** *adv.,* to the place where
     Aeneas: Aeneas, Aeneae, *m.,* Aeneas, mythological ancestor of the Romans, who fuses the Trojan story with the Roman story
     Tullus: Tullus, Tulli, *m.,* Tullus Hostilius, the third king of Rome, noted for his wealth; the verb *deciderunt* is understood with the subjects Aeneas, Tullus and Ancus. **dives: dives, divitis,** *adj.,* rich, wealthy
     Ancus: Ancus, Anci, *m.,* Ancus Martius, the fourth king of Rome, perhaps included as an example of how death can strike a royal without money as well as one with money.

16 **pulvis: pulvis, pulveris,** *m.,* dust; **umbra: umbra, umbrae,** *f.,* shadow

17 **scit: scio, scire, scivi, scitum,** know; **adiciant: adicio, adicere, adieci, adiectum,** add
     hodiernae: hodiernus, -a, -um, *adj.,* today's
     crastina: crastinus, -a, -um, *adj.,* tomorrow's; **summa: summa, summae,** *f.,* sum

19 **cuncta: cunctus, -a, -um,** *adj.,* (used substantively) all
     manus: manus, manus, *f.,* hand; **avidas: avidus, -a, -um,** *adj.,* eager, greedy
     fugient: fugio, fugere, fugi, fugiturum, escape; **heredis: heres, heredis,** *m.,* heir

20 **amico ... animo:** (with *dare)* give to one's very own dear soul

21 **semel: semel,** *adv.,* once; **occideris: occido, occidere, occidi, occasum,** die
     splendida: splendidus, -a, -um, *adj.,* stately, august; this is an epithet transferred from Minos to his decision; **Minos: Minos, Minois,** *m.,* Minos, king of Knossos on Crete, later a judge in the lower world

22 **arbitria: arbitrium, arbitri(i),** *n.,* judgment (poetic plural); *dare arbitria =* "to pass judgment"

23 **Torquate: Torquatus, Torquati,** *m.,* perhaps Torquatus Manlius, a member of the gens Manlia, famous for a family ancestor who wrested a torques, a common twisted necklace, from a defeated Gaul
     genus: genus, generis, *n.,* family; **facundia: facundia, facundiae,** *f.,* eloquence

24 **restituet: restituo, restituere, restitui, restitutum,** restore (to life)
     pietas: pietas, pietatis, *f.,* piety, uprightness

25 **infernis: infernus, -a, -um,** *adj.,* infernal, of the lower world; **tenebris: tenebrae, tenebrarum,** *f. pl.,* darkness; **Diana: Diana, Dianae,** *f.,* Diana, virgin goddess of the hunt; **pudicum: pudicus, -a, -um,** *adj.,* chaste

nos ubi decidimus

quo pater Aeneas, quo Tullus dives et Ancus,   15

    pulvis et umbra sumus.

quis scit an adiciant hodiernae crastina summae

    tempora di superi?

cuncta manus avidas fugient heredis, amico

    quae dederis animo.   20

cum semel occideris et de te splendida Minos

    fecerit arbitria,

non, Torquate, genus, non te facundia, non te

    restituet pietas;

infernis neque enim tenebris Diana pudicum   25

    liberat Hippolytum,

nec Lethaea valet Theseus abrumpere caro

    vincula Perithoo.

26 **liberat: libero, liberare, liberavi, liberatum,** free

  Hippolytum: Hippolytus, Hippolyti, *m.,* Hippolytus, son of Theseus, devoted to hunting and Diana; he rejected the advances of his stepmother, Phaedra; after her suicide, his father Theseus banished him, thinking that he had raped or attempted to rape Phaedra. At the request of Theseus, Poseidon stirred up waves along the shore where Hippolytus was driving his chariot. The horses of this chariot reared up, throwing off their driver whom they trampled to death.

27 **Lethaea: Lethaeus, -a, -um,** *adj.,* Lethaean, of or belonging to the River Lethe, the river of forgetfulness, in the lower world

  valet: valeo, valere, valui, have power, be well, be strong

  Theseus: Theseus, Thesei, *m.,* Theseus, king of Athens

  abrumpere: abrumpo, abrumpere, abrupi, abruptum, break away, break free

28 **vincula: vinculum, vinculi,** *n.,* chain

  Perithoo: Perithous, Perithoi, *m.,* Perithous, friend of Theseus, punished for attempting to carry off Proserpina, wife of Hades (god of the underworld); both heroes were chained in the underworld but Hercules saved Theseus; Theseus, after his own death, saw Perithous again in the underworld; imprisoned in the Lethe, the river of forgetfulness, Perithous had forgotten what Theseus could not forget.

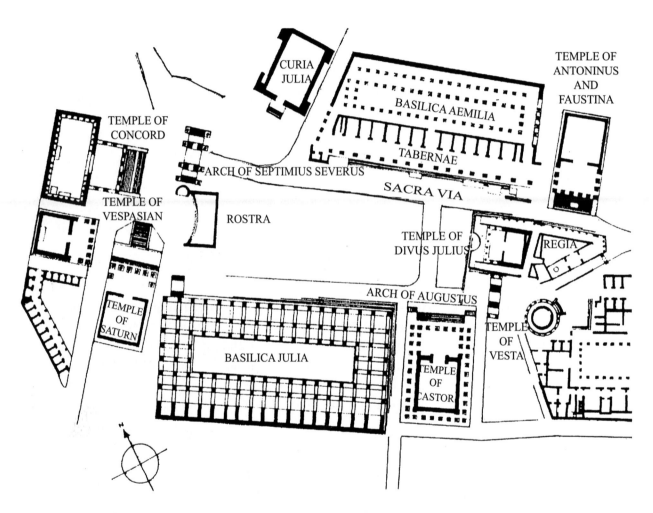

The above illustration shows the Roman Forum near the end of the republic. This area was a confluence of roads and a meeting place for people. Catullus (Poem 10) refers to meeting friends in the busy square, and Horace (*Sermones* I.9) encounters his garrulous companion somewhere in the center of the Forum as he is making his way toward the Temple of Vesta.

The view above presents the remains of the Basilica Julia, a building used in the Augustan era primarily for matters of court. Earlier basilicas were constructed in the Forum and bear testimony to the widespread use of public space for legal processes.

Sermones I.9

1   **ibam forte:** "I was walking by chance," i.e., "I happened to be walking"
     sicut, *conj.,* as, just as; **mos: mos, moris,** *m.,* way, custom

2   **nescio quid: nescio quid,** *indef. pron.,* something or other
     meditans: meditor, meditari, meditatus sum, think over, consider
     nugarum: nugae, nugarum, *f. pl.,* trifles, nonsense
     totus: totus, a, -um, *adj.,* whole, entire; Horace is saying that he was completely
       absorbed in his thoughts *(illis).*

3   **accurrit: accurro, accurrere, accurri, accursum,** run up to
     arrepta: arripio, arripere, arripui, arreptum, seize, lay hold of; grab

4   **quid agis:** a conventional greeting, "How are you?"
     dulcissime rerum: term of endearment or affection, "you, sweetest of things," which
       means effectively, "you, most delightful man in the world"

5   **suaviter: suaviter,** *adv.,* very well
     et cupio omnia quae vis: a standard Roman phrase amounting to "I hope the best
       for you."

6   **adsectaretur: assector, assectari, assectatus sum,** accompany, keep following
     num quid: num quid = numquid, *adv.,* (to introduce direct question) "There's
       nothing you want, is there?"
     occupo: occupo, occupare, occupavi, occupatum, seize, break; break in

7   **noris = noveris: nosco, noscere, novi, notum,** get to know, know, be familiar
       with
     pluris: plus, pluris, *adj.,* more; used as a substantive in the genitive case showing
       value; "You will be to me of more value because of this," i.e., "You will be worth
       more to me because of this."

8   **misere: misere,** *adv.,* desperately
     discedere: discedo, discedere, discessi, discessum, get away, depart
     quaerens: quaero, quaerere, quaesivi, quaesitum, try

9   **modo: modo,** *adv.,* sometimes; **interdum: interdum,** *adv.,* sometimes
     The infinitives *ire, consistere, dicere* (line 10) are historical infinitives used instead
       of the imperfect indicative form of the verb.
     consistere: consisto, consistere, constiti, come to a stop, pause, halt

10   **puero: puer, pueri,** *m.,* slave (whether young or old); this is a dative of reference
       instead of a genitive of possession.
     sudor: sudor, sudoris, *m.,* sweat

11   **manaret: mano, manare, manavi, manatum,** flow, run

Horace's first Book of Satires, published in 35 B.C., was his first published literary work. Its ten satires, composed in dactylic hexameters, are a collection of conversations entitled *Sermones.* Their language is informal and colloquial. They anticipate the careful craftsmanship of the *Odes,* published twelve years later. Whereas the content of an ode tends to be philosophical or reflective, the *Sermones* deal with everyday topics such as daily life in Rome, travel, dining, parenting, education, governance, and family.

Sermones I.9, set in the Forum Romanum in downtown Rome, relates the poet's chance meeting with a garrulous bore, who wants to be introduced to Horace's friend Maecenas. There are several speakers. To facilitate the reader's comprehension of who is speaking and when, I have used the following system: all remarks in *italics* are those attributed to the garrulous bore; the lines in **boldface** to Horace; the underlined to Aristius Fuscus, a friend of Horace who arrives unexpectedly later in the narrative; the ***italicized*** and ***boldfaced*** to the unnamed bailbondsman who also suddenly appears in hot pursuit of the bore.

Ibam forte via Sacra, sicut meus est mos,
nescio quid meditans nugarum, totus in illis.
accurrit quidam notus mihi nomine tantum,
arreptaque manu *quid agis, dulcissime rerum?*
'suaviter, ut nunc est,' inquam, **'et cupio omnia quae vis.'**
cum adsectaretur, **'num quid vis?'** occupo. at ille
'noris nos' inquit; *'docti sumus.'* hic ego **'pluris**
hoc' inquam **mihi eris.'** misere discedere quaerens,
ire modo ocius, interdum consistere, in aurem
dicere nescio quid puero, cum sudor ad imos   10
manaret talos. **'o te, Bolane, cerebri**

11 **talos: talus, tali,** *m.,* the anklebone, ankle; *ad imos talos,* "to my very ankles"
   Bolane: Bolanus, -a, -um, *adj.,* of or belonging to the town of Bola (an ancient town of the Aequi in Latium)
   cerebri: cerebrum, cerebri, *n.,* brain, understanding; attitude on life; the genitive case expresses the respect in which the person is *felicem,* an accusative of exclamation; "fortunate in your brain," i.e., "How lucky you are to have such a temperament!"

12 **aiebam: aio,** (defective verb, always used to introduce direct statements) say, affirm; the imperfect form suggests repeated action.

   tacitus: tacitus, -a, -um, *adj.,* silent (used adverbially here); "I kept saying silently," or "I kept saying to myself."

   quidlibet: quislibet-quidlibet, *indef. pron.,* anything; with *garriet* (line 13) the sense seems to be, "He chattered about anything and everything!"

13 **garriret: garrio, garrire, garrivi, garritum,** chatter, talk

   vicos: vicus, vici, *m.,* street; houses on both sides of a road or highway, hence a village; in a city, a block, a street including the houses on each side

15 **iamdudum: iamdudum,** *adv.,* for some time; with a present tense, the meaning is that of the English present perfect, "have been"; "I have been noticing that for some time."

   nil agis: a colloquial expression, "you are doing nothing," i.e., "Nothing of the kind!"

   usque: usque, *adv.,* all the way

16 **opus est:** an idiom meaning "there is need of" (with ablative)

17 **circumagi: circum+ago, agere, egi, actum,** take out of one's way; here the sense is, "There is no need for you to be taken out of your way."

   quendam: quidam, quaedam, quiddam, *indef. pron.,* a certain person, someone

   visere: viso, visere, visi, visum, visit, call on

18 **cubat: cubo, cubare, cubui, cubitum,** lie down, recline, be in bed; the implication is that the person whom Horace is visiting is sick in bed.

   hortos: hortus, horti, *m.,* garden; perhaps the plural forms mean "park"; Caesar willed his "gardens" to the Romans; these were situated on the Janiculum Hill just across the Tiber. They were the objective of Horace's excursion on foot.

19 **nil habeo quod agam** = "I have nothing to do"

   piger: piger-pigra-pigrum, *adj.,* sluggish, slow, lazy

20 **demitto: demitto, demittere, demisi, demisssum,** lower, drop, droop

   auriculas: auricula, auriculae, *f.,* the ear

   iniquae: inquus, -a, -um, *adj.,* unequal, here "stubborn"

   asellus: asellus, aselli, *m.,* ass

21 **dorso: dorsum, dorsi,** *n.,* back (ablative of means)

   subiit: subeo, subire, subii or subivi, subitum, (with ablative of means) go under; "when it (the ass) is bearing too heavy a load on its back"

   onus: onus, oneris, *n.,* burden, load, weight

felicem!' aiebam tacitus, cum quidlibet ille
garriret, vicos, urbem laudaret. ut illi
nil respondebam, 'misere cupis' inquit 'abire;
iamdudum video: sed nil agis; usque tenebo;
persequar hinc quo nunc iter est tibi.' **'nil opus est te** 15
circumagi: quendam volo visere non tibi notum:
trans Tiberim longe cubat is, prope Caesaris hortos.'
'nil habeo quod agam et non sum piger; usque sequar te.'
demitto auriculas, ut iniquae mentis asellus,   20
cum gravius dorso subiit onus, incipit ille:
'si bene me novi non Viscum pluris amicum,
non Varium facies; nam quis me scribere pluris
aut citius possit versus? quis membra movere
mollius? invideat quod et Hermogenes ego canto.'   25
interpellandi locus hic erat: **'est tibi mater,**
cognati, quis te salvo est opus?' 'haud mihi quisquam:
omnis composui.' **'felices! nunc ego resto.**

---

22 **si bene me novi:** colloquial expression meaning "if I know me"
    Viscum: Viscus, Visci, *m.,* Viscus (an unknown friend of Horace)
    amicum: a noun in apposition with Viscum

23 **Varium: Varius, Vari(i),** *m.,* Varius (an unknown friend of Horace)
    pluris: (genitive of value) of more, worth more

25 **mollius: mollius** *adv.,* more gracefully
    invideat: invideo, invidere, invidi, invisum, envy
    et: et, *adv.,* even
    Hermogenes: Hermogene, Hermogenis, *m.,* Hermogenes, a singer contemporary
        with Horace; translate in this order, *et Hermogenes invideat quod ego canto.*

26 **interpellandi: interpello, interpellare,** interrupt (a speaker)

27 **cognati: cognatus, -a, -um,** *adj.,* related by blood; (substantive) relative(s)
    quis = quibus
    salvo: salvus, -a, -um, *adj.,* safe, unhurt, well
    est opus: Horace asks whether there is anybody who needs the bore alive, i.e. "Do
        you have anybody whose well-being depends on your survival?"

28 **composui: compono, componere, composui, compositum,** lay out (for burial),
        put to rest
    resto: resto, restare, restiti, survive, remain

29 **confice: conficio, conficere, confeci, confectum,** finish off (supply *me);* the
  implication is that he had talked his relatives to death.
  instat: insto, instare, institi, draw near
  fatum: fatum, fati, *n.,* fate
  triste: tristis-triste, *adj.,* sad
  Sabella: Sabellus, -a, -um, *adj.,* Sabine; interest in prophecy characterized the
  Sabines.

30 **puero:** dative in apposition with *mihi* (understood)
  cecinit: cano, canere, cecini, cantum, sing; (with diviners) foretell, prophesy
  anus: anus, anus, *f.,* an old woman
  divina … mota … urna: (ablative absolute) "as the divining urn was shaken"

31 **dira: dirus, -a, -um,** *adj.,* dire, deadly
  venena: venenum, veneni, *n.,* poison
  hosticus: hosticus, -a, -um, *adj.,* hostile, enemy's
  auferet: aufero, auferre, abstuli, ablatum, carry off, kill

32 **laterum: latus, lateris,** *n.,* side, lung; *dolor laterum,* pleurisy
  tussis: tussis, tussis, *f.,* cough
  tarda: tardus, -a, -um, *adj.,* slow, crippling
  podagra: podagra, podagrae, *f.,* arthritis in the foot

33 **garrulus: garrulus, -a, -um,** *adj.,* talkative, chattering, babbling
  consumet: consumo, consumere, consumpsi, consumptum, spend, destroy
  quando … cumque: tmesis for **quandocumque,** *adv.,* at some time or other
  loquaces: loquax, loquacis, *adj.,* babbling, talkative; used substantively to mean
  "a chatterbox"

34 **sapiat: sapio, sapere, sapivi** or **sapii,** be discerning, be wise
  vitet: vito, vitare, vitavi, vitatum, avoid
  simul atque: simul atque, *conj.,* as soon as
  adoleverit: adolesco, adolescere, adolevi, grow up, come to maturity
  aetas: aetas, aetatis, *f.,* age, life

35 **Ventum erat:** This impersonal verb form means essentially "We arrived." This line
  seems to act like a curtain being raised on Scene II of a short play. Act I of the
  journey has taken place along the Sacra Via. The residence of Maecenas where
  Horace probably was living (lines 48-52) was on the Esquiline Hill. Horace
  and the bore come to a stop in the vicinity of the Temple of Vesta in the Forum
  Romanum (line 35). Suddenly (lines 36-37) the bore remembers that he has to be
  in court. Perhaps proximity to the Basilica Julia prompted this recollection.
  quarta … parte: quarta pars, quartae partis, *f.,* one fourth

confice; namque instat fatum mihi triste, Sabella   *2nd sg pres act imp*
quod puero cecinit divina mota anus urna: *hyperbaton* 30
hunc neque dira venena nec hosticus auferet ensis,   *nom subj*
nec laterum dolor aut tussis, nec tarda podagra;   *gen poss* *nom subj*
garrulus hunc quando consumet cumque: loquaces,   *nom subj*
si sapiat, vitet, simul atque adoleverit aetas.'   *nom subj*
ventum erat ad Vestae, quarta iam parte diei   ?35 *abl abs*
praeterita, et casu tunc respondere vadato   *participle perf (fs)*
debebat; quod ni fecisset, perdere litem.   *3rd sg plup act subjunc*
'si me amas' inquit 'paulum hic ades.' 'interéam si   *adv*
aut valeo stare aut novi civilia iura;   *compl inf*
et propero quo scis.' 'dubius sum quid faciam' inquit,   40
'tene relinquam an rem.' 'me, sodes.' 'non faciam' ille,   *1st sg fut act ind*

tmesis

---

36 **praeterita: praetereo, praeterire, praeterivi** or **praeterii, praeteritum,** go by, pass by; **casu: casus, casus,** *m.,* chance
respondere: respondeo, respondere, respondi, responsum, answer a summons, to appear in court
vadato: vador, vadari, vadatus sum, put up bail; a person who puts up security money for a defendant in a case to guarantee the presence of that defendant in court at the appointed time of the session; here an ablative absolute, "since bail had been paid"

37 **perdere : perdo, perdere, perdidi, perditum,** destroy, do away with, waste
litem: lis, litis, *f.,* a lawsuit, case

38 **si me amas:** colloquial expression for "please."
interéam: intereo, interire, interii, interitum, be lost, perish; "may I perish if …", a colloquial expression for "I'd be darned if …"
ades: adsum, adesse, adfui, be beside, help; this is the technical term meaning to give support by one's presence in court, to appear as an advocate; *ades* is the second person singular imperative form of the verb; Horace's subsequent remarks imply that the bore's command was for Horace to accompany him into the courtroom as an advocate.

39 **valeo: valeo, valere, valui,** be strong, be able, have the strength; Horace gives three reasons for refusing: 1) he is not strong enough to stand that long; 2) he knows nothing about civil law; 3) he has other business.

40 **propero: propero, properare, properavi, properatum,** hasten, rush
dubius: dubius, -a, -um, *adj.,* doubtful, not sure

41 **tene = te +ne; ne** is the suffix indicating a question; **rem = litem** = "my case"   *syncope / apocope*
sodes: sodes = si audes (uncontracted form) "if you please me," "please"

42 **praecedere: praecedo, praecedere, praecessi, praecessum,** go in front, lead the
way
coepit: coepi, coepisse, coepi, begin
contendere … cum victore: "to fight a champion"

syncope

44 **hinc: hinc,** *adv.,* after this
repetit: repeto, repetere, repetivi, repetitum, return to, "go back on the attack";
hominum = amicorum; bene = vere
mentis bene sane: "of good judgment"

45 **dexterius: dexterius,** *adv.,* more skillfully
usus: utor, uti, usus sum, (with the ablative) use, make use of

46 **adiutorem: adiutor, adiutoris,** *m.,* supporter, helper
secundas: secundus, -a, -um, *adj.,* secondary; *partes* (role) is understood; *secundas
partes ferre,* play a secondary role; The reference is to someone in drama who
is willing to take up a role second to that of the actor who has a primary role.

47 **velles: volo, velle, volui,** be willing
tradere: trado, tradere, tradidi, traditum, introduce
dispeream: dispereo, disperire, disperii, perish, be destroyed, die; this is another
colloquial expression, "I'll be darned."

syncope

48 **summosses = submovisses: submoveo, submovere, submovi, submotum,** put out
of the way, drive off, send away, remove
omnes: refers to all the other people that Horace would move away so that the bore
would have immediate access to Maecenas.
isto: iste-ista-istud, *adj.,* that (with a pejorative connotation)
illic: illic, *adv.,* in that place

49 **quo:** the antecedent is *isto … modo* (in lines 48-49)
rere: reor, reri, ratus sum, think; *rere = reris*
purior: *comp. adj.* from **purus, -a, -um,** *adj.,* pure, innocent

50 **aliena: alienus, -a, -um,** *adj.,* foreign, strange; (with ablative) free from
malis: malum, mali, *n.,* evil, problem
officit: officio, officere, offeci, offectum, (with dative) block, impede, get in the way of,
bother

51 **ditior: dis, ditis,** *adj.,* wealthy, rich
quia: quia, *conj.,* because (of the fact that), the fact that; the *quia* clause is the subject
of *officit.*
doctior: doctus, -a, -um, *adj.,* learned

52 **atqui: atqui,** *conj.,* but, nevertheless, and yet

et praecedere coepit. ego, ut <u>contendere</u> durum est   *[comp] pres act inf*

cum <u>victore</u>, sequor. '*Maecenas quomodo tecum?*' *abl accom*

hinc repetit: '*paucorum hominum et mentis bene sanae;*   *partitive gen*

nemo dexterius fortuna est usus. haberes   *nom, abl*   **45**

magnum adiutorem, <u>posset</u> qui ferre secundas,   *3s imp act subjunc*

hunc hominem velles si <u>tradere</u>: dispeream ni   *compl pres act inf*

summosses omnis.' '**non isto vivimus illic**   *2nd sg plup act subjunc*

quo tu <u>rere</u> modo; domus hac nec purior ulla est   *2nd sg pres dep*

nec magis <u>his</u> aliena <u>malis</u>; nil mi officit' **inquam**   **50**

'**<u>ditior</u> hic aut est quia <u>doctior</u>; est locus <u>uni</u>**   *adj cuique*

cuique suus.' '*magnum narras, vix credibile.*' '**atqui**   *dat, nom*

sic habet.' '**accendis, quare cupiam magis <u>illi</u>**   *dat (io?)   nom*

proximus esse.' '**velis tantummodo, quae tua virtus,**   *adv pos*

expugnabis; et est qui vinci possit, eoque   *compl inf pres pass*   **55**

difficilis <u>aditus</u> primos habet.' '*haud mihi <u>deero</u>:*   *1sg fut act ind*

<u>muneribus</u> servos corrumpam; non, hodie si   *abl means*

exclusus fuero, desistam; <u>tempora</u> quaeram;   *acc do*

---

53 **sic (se res) habet:** that's the situation

accendis: accendo, accendere, accendi, accensum, set on fire; inflame (me) with reasons why; **quare: quare,** *interrogative adv.,* why

54 **tantummodo: tantum modo,** *adv.,* merely, only, just

virtus: virtus, virtutis, *f.,* courage (used sarcastically); note the combative connotations of words in lines 53-56.

55 **expugnabis: expugno, expugnare, expugnavi, expugnatum,** overcome, take by storm

eoque: eo(que), *adv.,* consequently, and for that reason

56 **habet = facit;** the sense seems to be, "Consequently he makes first approaches difficult."; **haud: haud,** *adv.,* not

deero: desum, deesse, defui, (with dative) sell oneself short, fail, let down

57 **muneribus: munus, muneris,** *n.,* gift, favor, bribe

corrumpam: corrumpo, corrumpere, corrupi, corruptum, bribe

58 **exclusus: excludo, excludere, exclusi, exclusum,** shut out, deny entry; the perfect participle passive appears with the future perfect form of the verb "to be," an older (perhaps more formal or dramatic) way of saying *exclusus ero.*

desistam: desisto, desistere, destiti, cease, give up

tempora quaeram: tempora quaerere, look for opportunities, bide one's time

59 **occurram: occurro, occurrere, occurri, occursum,** meet, confront; notice the rapid succession of verbs in lines 58-59 reflecting how the bore is a man of prompt "action" in self-interest, hardly pleasing to Horace.
    triviis: trivium, trivi(i), *n.,* meeting place of three roads, intersection

60 **haec dum agit:** "while he is carrying on this way"

61 **Fuscus Aristius:** Aristius Fuscus is Horace's friend adressed in *Odes* I.22.

62 **pulchre: pulchre,** *adv.,* beautifully, fully, splendidly, very well
    nosset = novisset
    consistimus: consisto, consistere, constiti, stop moving, come to a halt

63 **quo tendis?:** "Where are you headed?"
    vellere: vello, vellere, velli or **vulsi, vulsum,** pull at, tug at (supply *togam*)

64 **prensare: prenso, prensare, prensavi, prensatum,** grasp, clutch at
    lentissima: lentus, -a, -um, *adj.,* sluggish, slow to action, unresponsive
    nutans: nuto, nutare, nutavi, nutatum, nod with the head

65 **distorquens: distorqueo, distorquere, distorquesi, disquorsitum,** roll
    eriperet: eripio, eripere, eripui, ereptum, tear away, rescue
    salsus: salsus, -a, -um, *adj.,* witty, funny
    male salsus, with a perverted sense of humor

66 **dissimulare: dissimulo, dissimulare, dissimulavi, dissimulatum,** pretend not to notice; the historical infinitive is used here as also in *urere,* to take the place of a finite verb form.
    iecur: iecur, iecuris, *n.,* the liver
    urere: uro, urere, ussi, ustum, burn
    bilis: bilis, bilis, *f.,* bile, anger

67 **secreto … loqui:** "to speak privately"

69 **tricesima: trice(n)simus, -a, -um,** *adj.,* thirtieth
    sabbata: sabbata, sabbatorum, *n. pl.,* the Jewish sabbath; this reference is obscure and reflects the cleverness and ingenuity of Aristius Fuscus, whereby he seizes on a respectable, almost noble (ultimately humorous) way to avoid helping Horace out of his plight.
    vin = visne

70 **curtis: curtus, -a, -um,** *adj.,* circumcised
    Iudaeis: Iudaeus, -a, -um, *adj.,* Jewish; used substantively, "the Jews"
    oppedere: oppedo, oppedere, (vulgar) (with dative) break wind in the face of, fart at, insult

occurram in triviis; deducam. nil sine magno
vita labore dedit mortalibus.' haec dum agit, ecce   60
Fuscus Aristius occurrit, mihi carus et illum
qui pulchre nosset. consistimus. 'unde venis?' et
'quo tendis?' rogat et respondet. vellere coepi,
et prensare manu lentissima bracchia, nutans,
distorquens oculos, ut me eriperet. male salsus   65
ridens dissimulare: meum iecur urere bilis.
'certe nescio quid secreto velle loqui te
aiebas mecum.' 'memini bene, sed meliore
tempore dicam: hodie tricesima sabbata: vin tu
curtis Iudaeis oppedere?' 'nulla mihi' inquam   70
'religio est.' 'at mi: sum paulo infirmior, unus
multorum: ignosces: alias loquar.' huncine solem
tam nigrum surrexe mihi! fugit improbus ac me
sub cultro linquit. casu venit obvius illi
adversarius et 'quo tu turpissime?' magna   75

71 **religio: religio, religionis,** *f.,* religious awe, conscience, scruple
   at mi: "But I have."
   infirmior: infirmus, -a, -um, *adj.,* weak, infirm, sick
   unus multorum: "one of the many," "one of the ordinary crowd"

72 **ignosces: ignosco, ignoscere, ignovi, ignotum,** forgive; the future tense acts like
      a polite imperative here.
   alias: alias, *adv.,* at another time
   huncine = hunc(ne)
   solem: sol, solis, *m.,* sun

73 **surrexe = surrexisse: surgo, surgere, surrexi, surrectum,** rise into view, emerge
      beyond horizon
   improbus: improbus, -a, -um, *adj.,* bad, shameless; (substantively) "bad guy",
      "scoundrel"

74 **cultro: culter, cultri,** *m.,* knife; the word suggests that Horace envisions himself as
      a victim about to be sacrificed; "leaves me in a lurch"
   obvius: obvius, -a, -um, *adj.,* in the way of; with *venire, obvius* takes the dative
      and means "to run into someone".

75 **adversarius: adversarius, -a, -um,** *adj.,* hostile, contrary, unfavorable, "the
      opponent" or "plaintiff"
   turpissime: turpis-turpe, *adj.,* foul, disgusting; (used substantively) "you utter
      heel!"

inclamat voce, et *'licet antestari?'* ego vero ~~Nom~~
oppono auriculam. rapit in ius: clamor utrimque: ~~prep acc~~
undique concursus. sic me servavit Apollo. ~~adv loos~~

76 **inclamat: inclamo, inclamare, inclamavi, inclamatum,** shout at, scold, chide
licet: licet, licuit, licitum est, it is allowed, it is permitted
antestari: antestor, antestari, antestatus sum, be called as a witness

77 **oppono: oppono, opponere, opposui, oppositum,** offer
auriculam: auricula, auriculae, *f.,* ear; this refers to an old custom whereby the ear
    of a bystander could be touched by a litigant, making the bystander a witness.
rapit: rapio, rapere, rapui, raptum, seize, carry off, snatch, drag
ius: ius, iuris, *n.,* justice, (figuratively) court
utrimque: utrimque, *adv.,* on both sides

78 **undique: undique,** *adv.,* on all sides, from every quarter
concursus: concursus, concursus, *m.,* throng, mob, running together

Meters

Horace uses many different meters. In this text the following meters appear: the first, second, fourth, and fifth Asclepiadean, the Alcaic, the Sapphic, and the first Archilochian. The student must come to understand the way that meter augments meaning; the music and the sound(s) of words in the poem orchestrate the poem's meaning in a subtle, transcending way. In rendering the schemes of each meter for ease of learning, I have made a simpler division of feet than is really the case.

Asclepiadean

First Asclepiadean

For ease of scansion, the first Asclepiadean can be viewed as consisting of a spondee, two choriambs (a choriamb consists of four syllables of which the first is long followed by two short syllables, followed by one long syllable) and (usually) an iamb (version A); however the final syllable may be long or short *(syllaba anceps)*, as indicated by the question mark inserted as the final syllable in the standard way of marking such a line (version B); this sign ‖ indicates a metrical pause *(diaeresis)*:

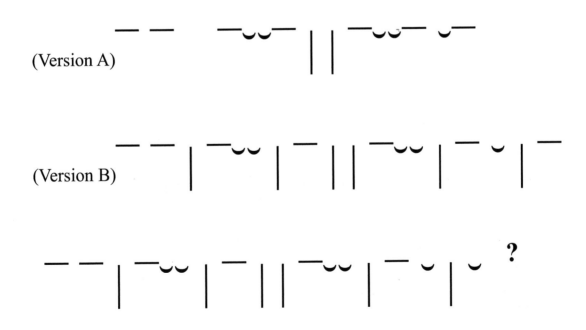

(Version A)

(Version B)

125

Second Asclepiadean

The second Asclepiadean consists of two lines; the first, called the Glyconic is the shorter of the two and consists of a spondee, a choriamb and (usually) an iamb (note that the final syllable can be long or short); the second line is a repeat of the first Asclepiadean line as shown above:

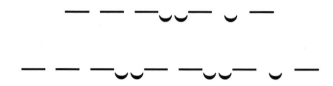

Fourth Asclepiadean

The fourth Asclepiadean is a quatrain whose first two lines are the first Asclepiadean; the third line is called a Pherecratean and consists of a spondee, a choriamb and a *syllaba anceps;* the final line is a Glyconic:

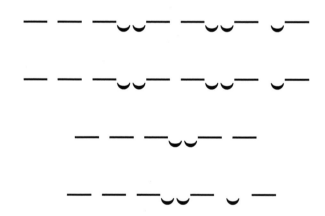

Fifth Asclepiadean

The fifth Asclepiadean adds a third choriamb to the first Asclepiadean; this meter is found in *Odes* I.11, I.18, and IV.10:

Alcaic

This is the meter most frequently used by Horace. The first and second line contain eleven syllables each. The first syllable of each line is a single syllable treated as one poetic foot; this is called anacrusis. The first syllable may be long or short, but in the poems covered by this text, the first syllable is always long. The anacrusis is followed by two trochees. These four syllables are called trochaic dipody. In the Greek Lyric poets, these four syllables almost always form two trochees, but Horace has regularly made the fifth syllable long. Thus the fifth syllable can theoretically be either long or short. The fourth foot is a dactyl, the fifth a trochee, and the sixth is a final syllable usually long in Horace. There is a short rest at the end of the line acting like the short syllable in a trochee. This pattern is repeated in the second line.

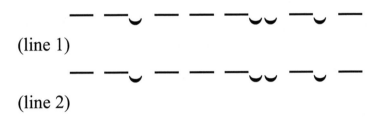

(line 1)

(line 2)

The third line begins with anacrusis (a single long or short syllable) followed by a trochee, a spondee, a trochee, a trochee or a spondee:

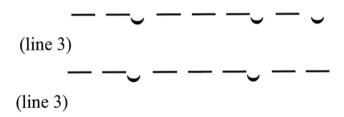

(line 3)

(line 3)

The fourth line consists of two dactyls, a trochee and a trochee or spondee:

(line 4)

(line 4)

Sapphic

The Sapphic meter derives its name from the Greek lyric poetry of the poetess Sappho, who wrote on the island of Lesbos in the sixth century B.C. The four lines observe a pattern which shows two variations. The first three lines have eleven syllables each. These syllables are grouped in two pairs of four syllables around the central three syllables of a dactyl. The fourth syllable and the eleventh syllable may be long or short. The pattern of the first three lines can be trochee, spondee or trochee, dactyl, trochee, trochee or spondee.

$$\text{—} \; \cup \; \text{—} \; \text{—} \; \text{—} \cup\cup \; \text{—} \; \cup \; \text{—} \; \text{—}$$

(lines 1-3)

The final line of the Sapphic is called an Adonic and consists of the last two poetic feet of the dactylic hexameter, namely a dactyl followed by a spondee or a troche:

$$\text{—}\cup\cup \; \text{—}\cup$$

(line 4)

Archilochian

The first Archilochian meter in its simplest and most straightforward forms consists of one line of dactylic hexameter and one half of a dactylic pentameter line:

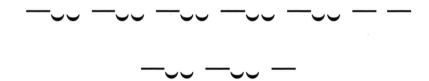

$$\text{—}\cup\cup \; \text{—}\cup\cup \; \text{—}$$

Figures of Speech

Figures of speech must not be confused with parts of speech. The latter define the type of word being used, such as a noun, pronoun, adjective, adverb, verb, participle, preposition, conjunction. Figures of speech are so called because their presence in a line of prose or poetry tends to shape the line by lending some subtlety of sound or sense which enhances the meaning of the line. The following list offers examples from the poems contained in this book. The student should be able to recognize and identify the figure, as well as offer an explanation of how the figure(s) work(s) in general and how the figures add to the meaning of the text or context in which they are found.

Alliteration: a series of words which begin with the same letter; subdivisions include consonance and assonance.

> certat tergeminis tollere honoribus   (*Odes* I.1.8)

Tergeminis and *tollere* begin with the same letter and the sound of the initial "t" is signalled by the "-tat" in *certat*.

Anaphora: repetition of the same word:

> qui nunc te fruitur credulus aurea,
> qui semper vacuam, semper amabilem   (*Odes* I.5.9-10)

Qui and *semper* are repeated.

Anastrophe: placing the object of a preposition before rather than after that preposition's occurrence in the line:

> Aequam memento rebus in arduis
> servare mentem,...   (*Odes* II.3.1-2)

Rebus is the object of the preposition *in*.

Antithesis: the side by side placement of words opposite in meaning; this may also be called **contraposition:**

> Parcus deorum cultor et infrequens
> insanientis dum sapientiae
> consultus erro...   (*Odes* I.34.1-3)

Insanientis modifies *sapientiae*.

> valet ima summis
> mutare et insignem attenuat deus,
> obscura promens;   (*Odes* I.34.12-14)

Ima is placed beside its opposite *summis; insignem* beside its opposite.

attenuat; obscua stands beside its opposite *promens*. These examples help concretize the meaning of the experience which the poet seeks to convey in that they forced a reversal of his mind-set.

Apostrophe: the direct address of a person, place or thing as present when absent: Horace will frequently address people in his poems to be receivers of his advice; this creates the illusion of their presence:

> Quis multa gracilis te puer in rosa
> perfusus liquidis urget odoribus
> grato, Pyrrha, sub antro?   (*Odes* I.5.1-3)

Pyrrha is addressed as if she were present.

Assonance: repetition of similar vowel sounds either medial or final:

> quid sit futurum cras fuge quaerere et
> quem Fors dierum cumque dabit lucro
> appone, nec dulcis amores
> sperne puer neque tu choreas,
> donec virenti canities abest
> morosa. .....   (*Odes* I.9.13-18)

In lines 13 and 14 the final "um" in *futurum* and *dierum* is echoed in *cumque* in line 14; the sound of "e" in *appone, amores, sperne, puer, neque. choreas, donec, canities* and *abest* shows both medial and final assonance in a poignant manner consistent with the highly charged feelings which the poet conveys in these lines.

Asyndeton: the absence of connectives between words, clauses, phrases:

> Nunc est bibendum, nunc pede libero
> pulsanda tellus, nunc Saliaribus
> ornare pulvinar deorum
> tempus erat dapibus, sodales.   (*Odes* I.37.1-4)

No connectives are expressed among the three key verbs; this reflects the highly excited emotional state of the author.

Chiasmus: an arrangement of pairs of words which, when written as separate lines, form the pattern A B B A; when lines are drawn connecting these common elements, the Greek letter X (chi) is formed; hence the term chiasmus denotes that formation:

> a   b   b   a
> vela dare atque iterare cursus   (*Odes* I.34.4)

Vela is the object of its following infinitive *dare; cursus* is the object of *iterare*.

Consonance: the repetition of the same consonantal sound medially or finally:

> vos Tempe totidem tollite laudibus (*Odes* I.21.9)

Tempe, totidem, tollite all begin with the consonant "t."

Ellipsis: the elimination of a word which is easily understood or derived from the context or from association with a nearby line:

> hunc, si mobilium turba Quiritium
> certat tergeminis tollere honoribus;
> illum, si proprio condidit horreo
> quidquid de Libycis verritur areis.   (*Odes* I.1.7-10)

Hunc and *illum* are governed by the verb *iuvat* (line 3) which has been omitted because it is understood by the reader or listener from the context of the lines.

Hendiadys: the use of two words with very similar meaning in order to assert one idea emphatically:

> post ignem aetheria domo
> subductum macies et nova febrium
> terris incubuit cohors   (*Odes* I.3.29-31)

Macies means disease and *febrium* means fevers; essentially they are the same thing in the context of the poem; Horace by hendiadys draws greater attention to the presence of sickness in the world because of man's acquisition of fire.

> cum tibi flagrans amor et libido,   (*Odes* I.25.13)

Amor and *libido* denote the lust of Lydia.

Homeoteleuton: a series of words which end in the same sounds:

> Integer vitae scelerisque purus
> non eget Mauris iaculis neque arcu
> nec venenatis gravida sagittis,
> Fusce, pharetra   (*Odes* I.22.1-4)

Mauris, iaculia, venatis, sagittis end in long *"-is."*

Hyperbole: extraordinary exaggeration:

> quo bruta tellus et vaga flumina,
> quo Styx et invisi horrida Taenari
> sedes Atlanteusque finis
> concutitur.   (*Odes* I.34.9-12)

Horace asserts that the clap of thunder and the flash of lightening which he saw scorched the earth and rivers, down through the underworld, all the way to Atlas. Somewhat of an overstatement!

Litotes: the assertion of something by denying its opposite:

> saevis Liburnis scilicet invidens
> privata deduci superbo
> non humilis mulier triumpho. (*Odes* I.37.30-33)

Non modifies *humilis* as Horace seeks to express Cleopatra's deep sense of arrogance in not wanting to be a part of a Roman triumph.

Metonymy: the use of one word to suggest another:

> metaque fervidis
> evitata rotis palmaque nobilis   (*Odes* I.1.4-5)

The *meta* literally refers to the two turn posts located at the ends of the *spina* in a Roman circus; this word suggests the chariot race which is the point of Horace's remark; similarly the word *palma* literally means the victory crown but symbolically means a victory in the chariot race.

Onomatopoeia: the matching of sound to sense:

> unde loquaces   (*Odes* III 13. 15-16)
> lymphae desiliunt tuae.

The predominance of "l" sounds and "a" and "e" combinations suggest the sound of the cascading, "talking" water of the fountain.

> cum fracta virtus, et minaces   (*Odes* II.7. 12-13)
> turpe solum tetigere mento.

The frequency of the harsh sounding "t" sounds out the actual fall of the poet onto his chin during the battle.

Personification: treating the inanimate as animate:

> O navis, referent in mare te novi
> fluctus! O quid agis? fortiter occupa   (*Odes* I.14.1-2)

Horace addresses the ship as if it is alive.

Polyptoton: repetition of key words with slight changes in the endings of the words:

> est ut viro vir latius ordinet
> arbusta sulcis... (*Odes* III.1.9)

Notice how *viro* is ablative and *vir* is nominative and they are placed beside one another.

Polysyndeton: the excessive use of connectives:

> Integer vitae scelerisque purus
> non eget Mauris iaculis neque arcu
> nec venenatis gravida sagittis,
> Fusce, pharetra,
> sive per Syrtis iter aestuosas   5
> sive facturus per inhospitalem
> Caucasum vel quae loca fabulosus
> lambit Hydaspes.   (*Odes* I.22.2-7)

These lines abound with connectives; *-que* on *scelerisque* (line 2), *neque* (line 3); the connectives *nec* (line 4), *sive* (lines 5, 6) and *vel* (line 7). The uses of many such connectives enlarges the impact of the enumeration which the poet is attempting to make.

Rhetorical Question: a question which does not expect an answer:

> Quis multa gracilis te puer in rosa
> perfusus liquidis urget odoribus
> grato, Pyrrha, sub antro?   (*Odes* I.5.1-3)

No answer is expected for this question which engages the reader or listener immediately; this is generally the intention of Horace when he uses rhetorical question.

Synchysis: an arrangement of pairs of words which, when written as separate lines, forms the pattern A B A B; the parallel nature of the connection of these common elements leads to the term parallel word order:

>   a   b   a   b
> Maecenas atavis edite regibus   (*Odes* I.1.1)

Maecenas is in the vocative case modified by *edite; atavis* modifies *regibus.*

Syncopation or **Syncope:** the contraction of words such as the genitive plural of the second declension, the third person plural of the perfect indicative active, or the second person singular perfect subjunctive active:

> Tu ne quaesieris, scire nefas, quem mihi, quem tibi
> finem di dederint, Leuconoe, nec Babylonios
> temptaris numeros. ...   (*Odes* I.11.1-3)

Quaesieris is the contracted form of *quaesiveris; temptaris* is the contracted form of *temptaveris.*

Synecdoche: a part of something which is used to suggest the whole *(pars pro toto):*

> Caecubum et prelo domitam Caleno
> tu bibes uvam: mea nec Falernae
> temperant vites neque Formiani
> pocula colles.   *(Odes* I.20.9-12)

Horace uses *uvam, vites, colles* to suggest wine; *uvam* and *vites* are *partes pro toto* and exemplify synecdoche; *colles* (hills) is mytonymy for the wine-producing vines grown on the hills.

Tricolon: grouping adjectives, nouns, phrases or clauses in threes:

> linquenda tellus et domus et placens
> uxor ...   *(Odes* II.14.21-22)

Horace uses *tellus, domus* and *uxor* in a tricolon to dramatize what one must leave upon death.

Tmesis: division of words into two parts:

> garrulus hunc quando consumet cumque:
> *(Satires* I.9.33)

Here Horace splits the word quandocumque so that he may enact for the reader-listener the splitting effect which the unexpected and garrulous person has had.

VOCABULARY

A

ab omni parte: "in every respect" or "altogether."

abrumpo, abrumpere, abrupi, abruptum, break away, break free

abscindo, abscindere, abscidi, abscissum, cut off from, divide

absumo, absumere, absumpsi, absumptum, consume, drink up

accendo, accendere, accendi, accensum, set on fire

accipiter, accipitris, *m.,* hawk

accurro, accurrere, accurri, accursum, run up to

Achaemenius, -a, -um, *adj.,* Persian

Achilles, Achillis, *m.,* the great hero Achilles

Acroceraunia, Acrocerauniorum, *n. pl.,* a promontory in western Greece

actus, tactus, *m.,* touch

acutus, -a, -um, *adj.,* sharp, bitter

acutus, -a, -um, *adj.,* shrill

addo, addere, addidi, additum, add to

adfero, adferre, adtuli, allatum, cause, bring

adicio, adicere, adieci, adiectum, add

adimo, adimere, ademi, ademptum, take away from, deprive

adiutor, adiutoris, *m.,* supporter, helper

adolesco, adolescere, adolevi, grow up, come to maturity

adsum, adesse, adfui, be beside, help

adultus, -a, -um, *adj.,* mature, grown up

adurgeo, adurgere, press closely, pursue

adventus, adventus, *m.,* arrival

adversarius, -a, -um, *adj.,* hostile, contrary, unfavorable, "the opponent", "plaintiff"

Aegaeum, Aegaei, *n.,* the Aegean Sea

Aeneas, Aeneae, *m.,* Aeneas, mythological ancestor of the Romans

aeneus, -a, -um, *adj.,* bronze

Aeolides, Aeolidae, *m.,* Sisyphus, son of Aeolus

Aeolius, -a, -um, *adj.,* Aeolian, the dialect of Sappho and Alcaeus

aequus, -a, -um, *adj.,* even, balanced, level

aer, aeris, *m.,* fog, mist, air

aeratus, -a, -um, *adj.,* bronze plated, with bronze plated prows

aes, aeris, *n.,* bronze

aesculetum, aesculeti, *n.,* oak forest

aestas, aestatis, *f.,* summer

aestivus, -a, -um, *adj.,* summer

aestuosus, -a, -um, *adj.,* hot, sweltering, raging, troubled, seething

aetas, aetatis, *f.,* age, youth, time, life

aetherius, -a, -um, *adj.,* heavenly

aevum, aevi, *n.,* life, lifetime

Afer-Afra-Afrum, *adj.,* African

Africus, Africi, *m.,* the southwest wind

agito, agitare, agitavi, agitatum, shake, toss

agmen, agminis, *n.,* marching column; (in the plural) warfare

ago, agere, egi, actum, (with *vita)* spend (life), do, drive away

agrestis-agreste, *adj.,* rustic, wild; "of country-folk"

aio, (defective verb, always used to introducce direct statements) say, affirm

tacitus, -a, -um, *adj.,* silent

albus, -a, -um, *adj.,* white

Algidus, Algidi, *m.,* Mt. Algidus

alias, *adv.,* at another time

alienus, -a, -um, *adj.,* foreign, strange; (with ablative) free from

alius, -a, -ud, *adj.,* other, another

allaboro, allaborare, allaboravi, allaboratum, add to, embellish

almus, -a, -um, *adj.,* nourishing, kind, genial

alo, alere, alui, alitum, nurture

altius: *comp. adv,* from *altus, -a, -um, adj.,* high, lofty, tall

altum, alti, *n.,* the deep sea

amabilis-amabile, *adj.,* loving, beloved, worthy of love

amarus, -a, -um, *adj.,* bitter, (used substantively) "bitterness"

amice, *adv.,* gladly, with good will

amico ... animo: (with *dare)* give to one's very own dear soul

amoenus, -a, -um, *adj.,* pleasant, lovely

amoveo, amovere, amovi, amotum, steal

amplius, *adv.,* more

amplus, -a, -um, *adj.,* large

Ancus, Anci, *m.,* Ancus Martius, the fourth king of Rome

angiportus, angiportus, *m.,* alley

angulus, anguli, *m.,* nook, corner

angustus, -a, -um, *adj.,* harsh, pinching, narrow, stressful, critical

anima, animae, *f.,* spirit, life, soul

animosus, -a, -um, *adj.,* bold

animus, animi, *m.,* spirit, mind

antecedo, antecedere, antecessi, precede

antehac, *adv.,* previously

antenna, antennae, *f.,* rigging, yardarm

antestor, antestari, antestatus sum, be called as a witness

antrum, antri, *n.,* grotto, cave

anus, anus, *f.,* an old woman, old maid

aper, apri, *m.,* wild boar

apex, apicis, *m.,* tiara, crown

apium, api(i), *n.,* parsley

Apollo, Apollinis, *m.,* Apollo, god of the sun, poetry, prophesy

apparatus, apparatus, *m.,* luxury

appareo, apparere, apparui, apparitum, show oneself

appono, apponere, apposui, appositum, (with dative) put, place (before), reckon

aptus, -a, -um, *adj.,* (with dative) fit for

Aquilo, Aquilonis, *m.,* north wind
arbiter, arbitri, *m.,* master, master of ceremonies, controller, lord
arbitrium, arbitri(i), *n.,* control, will, decision, judgment
arbor, arboris, *f.,* tree
arbustum, arbusti, *n.,* orchard, tree
arbutus, arbuti, *f.,* strawberry tree
arcanus, -a, -um, *adj.,* secret
arceo, arcere, arcui, hold off, keep at a distance, keep away
Arcturus, Arcturi, *m.,* Arcturus, the brightest star of Bootes
arcus, arcus, *m.,* bow
ardeo, ardere, arsi, burn with passion
arduus, -a, -um, *adj.,* steep, difficult, harsh
area, areae, *f.,* an open public space, playground, threshing floor
arguo, arguere, argui, argutum, make known, prove, disclose
aridus, -a, -um, *adj.,* dry, parched
arripio, arripere, arripui, arreptum, seize, lay hold of, grab
arrogans, arrogantis, *adj.,* insolent, arrogant
artus, -a, -um, *adj.,* dense
asellus, aselli, *m.,* ass
asper-aspera-asperum, *adj.,* fierce, rough, roughened, dangerous
assector, assectari, assectatus sum, accompany, keep following
atavus, -a, -um, *adj.,* ancestral
ater-atra-atrum, *adj.,* black
Atlanteus, -a, -um, *adj.,* related to Atlas, the end of the then known world
Atlas, Atlantis, *m.,* the giant Atlas
atqui, *conj.,* (a very strong objection) but, nevertheless, and yet
Atrides, Atridae, *m.,* Agamemnon and Menelaus (sons of Atreus)
atrox, atrocis, *adj.,* savage, harsh, fierce
Attalicus, -a, -um, *adj.,* of Attalus
attenuo, attenuare, attenuavi, attenuatum, humble
Atticus, -a, -um, *adj.,* Attic, Greek
audax, audacis, *adj.,* impertinent, bold
audeo, audere, ausus sum, dare, venture
aufero, auferre, abstuli, ablatum, carry off, kill, take away, spoil
Aufidus, Aufidi, *m.,* a river in Apulia near Horace's birthplace
aula, aulae, *f.,* mansion, palace
aura, aurae, *f.,* breeze, wind
aureus, -a, -um, *adj.,* golden
auricula, auriculae, *f.,* ear
aurum, auri, *n.,* gold
Auster, Austri, *m.,* the south wind
autumnus, autumni, *m.,* autumn
avidus, -a, -um, *adj.,* eager, greedy
avis, avis, *f.,* bird
avitus, -a, -um, *adj.,* ancestral
avius, -a, -um, *adj.,* pathless, trackless

B

Babylonius, -a, -um, *adj.,* Babylonian (Chaldean) (famous for astrology)

bacchor, bacchari, bacchatus sum, revel, howl

Bandusia, Bandusiae, *f.,* a pleasant spring near Venusia, the birthplace of Horace

barbare, *adv.,* barbarously

barbitos, barbiti, *m.,* lyre; the accusative singular is *barbiton.*

beatus, -a, -um, *adj.,* happy, blessed

beo, beare, beavi, beatum, make happy

bibo, bibere, bibi, drink

bilis, bilis, *f.,* bile, anger, wrath

Bolanus, -a, -um, *adj.,* of or belonging to the town of Bola

bos, bovis, *f.,* ox

bracchium, bracchi(i), *n.,* arm

brevis-breve, *adj.,* short-lived

Brittanni, Brittannorum, *m. pl.,* the Britons (people of the Far West)

bruma, brumae, *f.,* (dead of) winter

Brutus, Bruti, *m.,* Brutus, the general at Philippi

brutus, -a, -um, *adj.,* inert, dull

C

cadus, cadi, *m.,* wine jar

Caecubum, Caecubi, *n.,* Caecuban wine (an expensive wine)

caedes, caedis, *f.,* carnage, slaughter

caelestis-caeleste, *adj.,* of or pertaining to the sky, heavenly

caelum, caeli, *n.,* heaven, the gates of heaven, sky, climate

caementum, caementi, *n.,* rubble, cement, foundation

Caesar, Caesaris, *m.,* Caesar Augustus

Calais, name of Lydia's boyfriend.

Calenus, -a, -um, *adj.,* of Cales, a town in northern Campania

caleo, calere, calui, be warm

callidus, -a, -um, *adj.,* clever

Camena, Camenae, *f.,* Muse, native goddess of Roman poetry; (figuratively) song

campus, campi, *m.,* (untilled) field, the Campus Martius

candeo, candere, candidi, candidum, shine, gleam

candidus, -a, -um, *adj.,* shining, white, clear

Canicula, Caniculae, *f.,* the Dog Star (Sirius), symbolic of intense summer heat

canities, canitiei, *f.,* grayness, old age

cano, canere, cecini, cantum, sing, (of diviners) foretell, prophesy

cantharus, canthari, *m.,* a tankard, a drinking vessel with large handles

canto, cantare, cantavi, cantatum, recite, sing

cantus, cantus, m. song

capax, capacis, *adj.,* capacious, full, spacious

capillus, capilli, *m.,* hair

Capitolium, Capitoli(i), *n.,* the Capitoline Hill (symbol of Rome)

caput, capitis *n.,* head, source

cardo, cardinis, *m.,* hinge
careo, carere, carui, caritum, (with ablative) be without, be free from, avoid
carina, carinae, *f.,* keel of a ship, hull
carpo, carpere, carpsi, carptum, pluck, pick, enjoy
casus, casus, *m.,* chance, fall, crash
catena, catenae, *f.,* chain
catulus, catuli, *m.,* puppy, hunting hound
catus, -a, -um, *adj.,* clever
Caucasus, Caucasi, *m.,* the Caucasus mountains
cautus, -a, -um, *adj.,* cautious
cavus, -a, -um, *adj.,* hollow
cebrius, -a, -um, *adj.,* drunk
cedo, cedere, cessi, cessum, leave, depart
celer, celeris, celere, *adj.,* quick, speedy, swift
cella, cellae, *f.,* storeroom, wine cellar
celsus, -a, -um, *adj.,* lofty
cena, cenae, *f.,* dinner, banquet
cerebrum, cerebri, *n.,* brain, understanding, attitude on life
Ceres, Cereris, *f.,* Ceres (the Greek Demeter), the goddess of grain
cereus, -a, -um, *adj.,* waxen, of wax; smooth and white as wax
certo, certare, certavi, certatum, vie, compete
certus, -a, -um, *adj.,* sure, dependable
cerva, cervae, *f.,* deer
cervix, cervicis, *f.,* neck
Chloe, Chloes, *f.,* Chloe, a Greek female name
chorea, choreae, *f.,* dance
chorus, chori, *m.,* band of dancers, dancing
ciborium, cibori(i), *n.,* goblet
cingo, cingere, cinxi, cinctum, surround, wreathe
circa, *adv.,* round about, around, near
circum+ago, agere, egi, actum, take out of one's way
cithara, citharae, *f.,* lyre
citius, *adv.,* sooner
citus, -a, -um, *adj.,* early, untimely, swift
clarus, -a, -um, *adj.,* famous, well known
classis, classis, *f.,* fleet
claudus, -a, -um, *adj.,* limping, halting, lame
clavis, clavis, *f.,* key
Cocytos, Cocyti, *m.,* Cocytos, the river of mourning in the underworld
coemo, coemere, coemi, coemptum, buy up
coepi, coepisse, coepi, begin
coerceo, coercere, coercui, coercitum, keep in order, herd
coetus, coetus, *m.,* crowd
cognatus, -a, -um, *adj.,* related by blood; (substantive) relative(s)
cogo, cogere, coegi, coactum, force, compel, bring together, gather, herd
cohibeo, cohibere, cohibui, hold, hold back

colligo, colligere, collegi, collectum, collect, gather
collis, collis, *m.,* hill
colo, colere, colui, cultum, take care of, cultivate, raise
colonus, coloni, *m.,* farmer, sharecropper
columba, columbae, *f.,* dove
coma, comae, *f.,* hair, (figuratively of persons) head, (of trees) foliage
combibo, combibere, combibi, drink in, drink up, absorb
committo, committere, commisi, commissum, commit, entrust
compello, compellere, compuli, compulsum, herd together, gather, collect
compesco, compescere, compescui, restrain, imprison
compono, componere, composui, compositum, lay out (for burial), put to rest
concha, conchae, *f.,* shell-shaped vessel, conch
concursus, concursus, *m.,* throng, mob, running together
concutio, concutere, concussi, concussum, shake
condicio, condicionis, *f.,* term, condition
condisco, condiscere, condidici, learn thoroughly
condo, condere, condidi, conditum, store up, hide
conficio, conficere, confeci, confectum, finish off
consisto, consistere, constiti, come to a stop, pause, halt, stand still
consocio, consociare, consociavi, consociatum, entwine, join
consularis-consulare, *adj.,* consular, consul's
consultus, -a, -um, *adj.,* (with genitive) adept in, expert in
consumo, consumere, consumpsi, consumptum, spend, destroy
contaminatus, -a, -um, *adj.,* polluted
contendere ... cum victore: "to fight a champion"
contendo, contendere, contendi, contentum, compete
contraho, contrahere, contraxi, contractum, contract, furl, take in
copula, copulae, *f.,* bond
cor, cordis, *n.,* heart
cornu, cornus, *n.,* horn
corona, coronae, *f.,* garland
corono, coronare, coronavi, coronatum, crown, wreathe
corrigo, corrigere, correxi, correctum, set straight, bring into order
corripio, corripere, corripui, correptum, hasten, quicken
corrumpo, corrumpere, corrupi, corruptum, bribe
cortex, corticis, *m./f.,* cork
coruscus, -a, -um, *adj.,* flashing
costum, costi, *n.,* perfume
Cragus, Cragi, *m.,* Mt. Cragus, a mountain in Lycia in Asia Minor
cras, *adv.,* tomorrow
crastinus, -a, -um, *adj.,* tomorrow's
creber-crebra-crebrum, *adj.,* frequent, repeated
credulus, -a, -um, *adj.,* (with dative) trusting, believing in confidently
cresco, crescere, crevi, cretum, increase, grow
cruentus, -a, -um, *adj.,* bloody
cubo, cubare, cubui, cubitum, lie down, recline, be in bed

culpo, culpare, culpavi, culpatum, blame, find fault with
culter, cultri, *m.,* knife
cultor, cultoris, *m.,* worshipper
cultus, cultus, *m.,* ways, manners
cumba, cumbae, *f.,* skiff, little boat
cunctus, -a, -um, *adj.,* whole, entire, (used substantively) all things
cupido, cupidinis, *m.,* desire (for gain)
cupressus, cupressi, *f.,* cypress tree
Cura, Curae, *f.,* Anxiety (a personification)
cura, curae, *f.,* anxiety
curo, curare, curavi, curatum, care
curriculum, curriculi, *n.,* racing chariot
currus, currus, *m.,* chariot
cursus, cursus, *m.,* course
curtus, -a, -um, *adj.,* circumcised
curvus, -a, -um, *adj.,* curved
Cyclades, Cycladum, *f. pl.,* the Cyclades
Cynthius, -a, -um, *adj.,* Cynthian
Cyprius, -a, -um, *adj.,* of the island of Cyprus, well known for shipbuilding
Cyprus, Cypri, *f.,* island of Cyprus

D

damno, damnare, damnavi, damnatum, condemn to
damnum, damni, *n.,* loss
Danaus, Danai, *m.,* king whose daughters killed their husbands
daps, dapis, *f.,* banquet, feast
Daunias, Dauniadis, *f.,* the province of Daunia (Apulia)
Daunus, Dauni, *m.,* Daunus, first king of Apulia
debeo, debere, debui, debitum, owe
debilito, debilitare, debilitavi, debilitatum, exhaust, weaken
decedo, decedere, decessi, decessum, withdraw, get off, disembark
decerto, decertare, decertavi, decertatum, struggle
decido, decidere, decidi, fall, descend, topple
decorus, -a, -um, *adj.,* adorned, fitting, proper, glorious, noble (confering *decus)*
decresco, decrescere, decrevi, decretum, diminish, subside, recede
decus, decoris, *n.,* glory
dedecet, dedecere, dedecuit, it is unfitting
dedico, dedicare, dedicavi, dedicatum, dedicate
deduco, deducere, deduxi, deductum, adapt, conduct, lead, escort
delenio, delenire, delenivi, delenitum, soothe, calm down
delibero, deliberare, deliberavi, deliberatum, resolve
Dellius, Delli(i), *m.,* Dellius
Delos, Deli, *f.,* the island of Delos
demens, dementis, *adj.,* mad
demitto, demittere, demisi, demisssum, lower, let down, drop, droop
demo, demere, dempsi, demptum, take away

dens, dentis, m., tooth
depono, deponere, deposui, depositum, put down, lay down
deproelior, deproeliari, deproeliatus sum, fight it out, battle fiercely
depromo, depromere, deprompsi, depromptum, bring out, take out
depropero, deproperare, deproperavi, deproperatum, prepare speedily, weave fast
deripio, deripere, deripui, dereptum, pull off, snatch away
descendo, descendere, descendi, descensum, descend
desero, deserere, deserui, desertum, abandon (the chase of), forsake
desiderium, desideri(i), n., longing, desire, grief, object of desire
desilio, desilire, desilui, desultum, leap down, jump down
desino, desinere, desii, desitum, cease
desisto, desistere, destiti, cease, give up
destino, destinare, destinavi, destinatum, be destined for, select, set apart
destringo, destringere, destrinxi, districtum, unsheathe
desum, deesse, defui, (with dative) sell oneself short, fail, let down
detestor, detestari, detestatus sum, detest
dexterius, adv., more skillfully
Diana, Dianae, f., Diana, virgin goddess of the hunt
dico, dicere, dixi, dictum, name, appoint
diduco, diducere, diduxi, diductum, draw apart, separate
Diespiter, Diespitris, m., old name for Jupiter, god of the sky
difficilis-difficile, adj., difficult, harsh, angry
diffugio, diffugere, diffugi, diffugiturum, flee in different directions, disappear
digitus, digiti, m., (index) finger
dignior: comp. adj., from dignus, -a, -um, adj., worthy
dignus, -a, -um, adj., (with ablative) worthy
dilectus, -a, -um, adj., beloved
diligo, diligere, dilexi, dilectum, prize
dimidium, dimidi(i), n., half
dimoveo, dimovere, dimovi, dimotum, move aside, remove
diota, diotae, f., a two-handled wine jug
diruo, diruere, dirui, dirutum, pull apart, destroy, wreck
dirus, -a, -um, adj., dire, deadly
discedo, discedere, discessi, discessum, get away, depart
dispereo, disperire, disperii, perish, be destroyed, die
displiceo, displicere, displicui, displicitum, (with dative) displease
dissimulo, dissimulare, dissimulavi, dissimulatum, pretend not to notice
dissociabilis-dissociabile, adj., dividing
dissolvo, dissolvere, dissolvi, dissolutum, break up, dispel
distorqueo, distorquere, distorsi, disquortum, roll
diva, divae, f., goddess
divello, divellere, divelli, divulsum, tear apart, tear to pieces
dives, divitis, adj., rich, wealthy
divitiae, divitiarum, f. pl., riches
divum, divi, n., the sky, open air
divus, -a, -um, adj., divine

divus, divi, *m.,* god

doctus, -a, -um, *adj.,* learned, versed in

doleo, dolere, dolui, dolitum, grieve, be in distress

dolum, doli, *n.,* deceit, trick

dominus, domini, *m.,* master, owner

domo, domare, domui, domitum, press, crush

domus, domus, *f.,* home, house

donec, *conj.,* while, as long as

dono, donare, donavi, donatum, honor by a gift, offer, give

dormio, dormire, dormivi, dormitum, sleep

dorsum, dorsi, *n.,* back (ablative of means)

dubius, -a, -um, *adj.,* doubtful, not sure

dulcis-dulce, *adj.,* nice, enjoyable, sweet

dulcissime rerum: term of endearment or affection, "sweetest of things"

dum, *conj.,* while (with historical present)

duro, durare, duravi, duratum, endure, withstand

durus, -a, -um, *adj.,* hard, difficult

E

edax, edacis, *adj.,* destructive, erosive

editus, -a, -um, *adj.,* sprung from

Edoni, Edonorum, *m. pl.,* Edonians

effundo, effundere, effudi, effusum, pour forth

egeo, egere, egui, (with ablative) need

eheu, *interj.,* what, Ah!, alas

elaboro, elaborare, elaboravi, elaboratum, develop, produce

emiror, emirari, emiratus sum, be amazed at

enavigo, enavigare, enavigavi, enavigatum, (root verb *navigo*) cross, sail across

ensis, ensis, *m.,* sword

eo(que), *adv.,* consequently, and for that reason

eo, ire, ii, itum, go, go by

eodem, *adv.,* to the same place

equa, equae, *f.,* mare

eques, equitis, *m.,* cavalryman, horseman, rider, knight

ergo, *adv.,* and so, then, therefore

eripio, eripere, eripui, ereptum, tear away, rescue

erro, errare, erravi, erratum, wander, stray (from the truth)

Erymanthus, Erymanthi, *m.,* Mt. Erymanthus in northern Arcadia

est ut = it is true that

et, *adv.,* also, even

Eurus, Euri, *m.,* Eurus, the east wind

eveho, evehere, evexi, evectum, raise up

evito, evitare, evitavi, evitatum, miss narrowly, graze

excludo, excludere, exclusi, exclusum, shut out, deny entry

excutio, excutere, excussi, excussum, cast aside, jilt

exeo, exire, exii, exitum, fly out

exigo, exigere, exegi, exactum, build up, erect, finish
expavesco, expavescere, expavi, dread
expedio, expedire, expedivi, expeditum, set aside
experior, experiri, expertus sum, test, try
expleo,, explere, explevi, expletum, fill up, fill to the brim
expugno, expugnare, expugnavi, expugnatum, overcome, take by storm
exstruo, exstruere, exstruxi, exstructum, heap up
exsul, exsulis, *m.,* expatriate

F

fabulosus, -a, -um, *adj.,* fabled
facilis-facile, *adj.,* easy, ready, easily impelled
facundia, facundiae, *f.,* eloquence
facundus, -a, -um, *adj.,* eloquent
Falernum, Falerni, *n.,* Falernian
Falernus, -a, -um, *adj.,* Falernian, a strong, superior wine
fallax, fallacis, *adj.,* deceptive, treacherous
fallo, fallere, fefelli, falsum, pass by unnoticed, slip by
fames, famis, *f.,* hunger
famulus, famuli, *m.,* servant, slave, worker
fastidio, fastidire, fastidivi, fastiditum, feel disgust for, shrink from, despise, shun
fastidiosus, -a, -um, *adj.,* (with genitive) scornful of, sick/tired/disdainful of
fatalis-fatale, *adj.,* deadly
fatum, fati, *n.,* fate
faveo, favere, favi, fauturus, -a, -um, (with *linguis*) abstain from ill-omened speech
fax, facis, *f.,* torch; (figuratively) flame, passion
febris, febris, *f.,* fever
fenestra, fenestrae, *f.,* window, shutter
ferio, ferire, strike
fero, ferre, tuli, latum, bring
ferocior: *comp. adj.* from *ferox, ferocis, adj.,* fierce, fierce spirited, defiant
ferus, -a, -um, *adj.,* wild, savage
ferveo, fervere, be boiling hot, boil, burn
fervidus, -a, -um, *adj.,* boiling, seething, turbulent, glowing
fessus, -a, -um, *adj.,* weary, weary from
festus, -a, -um, *adj.,* festive
fides, fidis, *f.,* chord, lyre
fido, fidere, fisus sum, (with dative) confide in, trust, believe
filum, fili, *n.,* thread
findo, findere, fidi, fissum, cleave, split
fio, fieri, factus sum, become, prove to be
flagrans, flagrantis, *adj.,* blazing, hot, flaming, burning
flavus, -a, -um, *adj.,* blond, yellow, (perhaps) sandy colored, golden
flebilis-flebile, *adj.,* (with dative) causing tears to, mourned by
fleo, flere, flevi, fletum, cry over, shed tears over, lament
flos, floris, *m.,* flower

fluctus, fluctus, *m.,* wave

flumen, fluminis, *n.,* river

fluvius, fluvi(i), *m.,* stream, river

focus, foci, *m.,* fireplace, hearth

folium, foli(i), *n.,* leaf

fons, fontis, *m.,* fountain, spring

Formianus, -a, -um, *adj.,* of Formiae, a town of Latium noted for its wine

formo, formare, formavi, formatum, form, transform

fors, fortis, *f.,* chance, fate

forsan, *adv.,* perhaps

fortis-forte, *adj.,* brave, courageous

fragilis-fragile, *adj.,* fragile, frail

frango, frangere, fregi, fractum, break, crush, maul, break up, while away

fraternus, -a, -um, *adj.,* brother's

fraus, fraudis, *f.,* deceit, theft

frequens, frequentis, *adj.,* crowded, densely packed

fretum, freti, *n.,* sea, surf, straight, (figuratively) waves

frigus, frigoris, *n.,* cold (associated with lack of passion or affection)

frons, frondis, *m., f.,* leaf, foliage

frons, frontis, *m.,* brow

fruges, frugum, *f. pl.,* crops

fruor, frui, fruitus/fructus sum, (with ablative) enjoy

frustra, *adv.,* in vain

fugax, fugacis, *adj.,* fleeing, hurrying

fugio, fugere, fugi, fugiturum, flee from, succeed in escaping from

fulgeo, fulgere, fulsi, shine, glitter, be conspicuous, be illustrious

fulgur, fulguris, *n.,* lightning

fundo, fundere, fudi, fusum, pour out

fundus, fundi, *m.,* farm, estate

funis, funis, *m.,* rope

funus, funeris, *n.,* funeral, destruction

furens, furentis, *adj.,* raging, wild

furio, furiare, (no perfect form), **furiatum,** drive mad, madden, infuriate

furiosus, -a, -um, *adj.,* furious

furo, furere, carouse, revel

furor, furoris, *m.,* fury, frenzy

furtim, *adv.,* secretly

furtum, furti, *n.,* trick, theft

Fuscus, Fusci, *m.,* Aristius Fuscus

G

Gaetulus, -a, -um, *adj.,* Gaetulian

garrio, garrire, garrivi, garritum, chatter, talk

garrulus, -a, -um, *adj.,* talkative, chattering, babbling

gaudeo, gaudere, gavisus sum, be glad, be pleased, rejoice in, delight in

gaza, gazae, *f.,* wealth

gelidus, -a, -um, *adj.,* chilly, cold

gelu, gelus, *n.,* icy coldness, frost, ice

geminus, -a, -um, *adj.,* twin

gemma, gemmae, *f.,* gem

gemo, gemere, gemui, gemitum, groan

genae, genarum, *f. pl.,* cheeks

genero, generare, generavi, generatum, beget, produce

generosior: *comp. adj.* from *generosus, -a, -um, adj.,* of high birth

generosius: *comp. adv.,* derived from *generosus, -a, -um, adj.,*noble

genu, genus, *n.,* knee

genus, generis, *n.,* race, family, (figuratively) son

Geryon, Geryonis, *m.,* Geryon, a giant with three bodies

Giganteus, -a, -um, *adj.,* of the giants

gracilis-gracile, *adj.,* slender

gradus, gradus, *m.,* step, approach

Graecus, -a, -um, *adj.,* Greek

Graius, -a, -um, *adj.,* Greek

gramen, graminis, *n.,* grass, grassy spot

grando, grandinis, *f.,* hail

Gratia, Gratiae, *f.,* a Grace, one of the three goddesses embodying charm and beauty

gratus, -a, -um, *adj.,* pleasing, attractive, welcome

gravidus, -a, -um, *adj.,* heavy

gravus, -a, -um, *adj.,* heavy

grex, gregis, *m.,* flock, herd

H

Hadria, Hadriae, *f.,* the Adriatic Sea

Haedus, Haedi, *m.,* Haedi, two stars in the wagoner (Auriga),

haedus, haedi, *m.,* a young goat, kid

Haemonia, Haemoniae, *f.,* Haemonia, the old name for Thessaly

hasta, hastae, *f.,* spear

haud, *adv.,* not

Hebrus, Hebri, *m.,* Hebrus, a river in Thrace

hedera, hederae, *f.,* ivy, sacred to Bacchus

Helena, Helenae, *f.,* Helen of Troy

heres, heredis, *m.,* heir

Hermogene, Hermogenis, *m.,* Hermogenes, a singer contemporary with Horace

heu, *interj.,* Alas! (Ah! is perhaps the modern equivalent.)

hiems, hiemis, *f.,* winter storm, winter

hinc, *adv.,* after this

hinnitus, hinnitus, *m.,* whinny

(h)in(n)uleus, (h)in(n)ulei, *m.,* fawn

Hippolytus, Hippolyti, *m.,* Hippolytus, son of Theseus

hodiernus, -a, -um, *adj.,* today's

hora, horae, *f.,* hour, time, the passing hour, season

horresco, horrescere, horrui, dread, become terrified at

horreum, horrei, *n.,* barn, granary
horridus, -a, -um, *adj.,* awful
hortus, horti, *m.,* garden
hospitalis-hospitale, *adj.,* friendly, hospitable
hosticus, -a, -um, *adj.,* hostile, enemy's
huc, *adv.,* hither, to this place
humilis-humile, *adj.,* submissive, humble
humus, humi, *f.,* ground
huncine = hunc(ne)
Hyades, Hyadum, *f.,* Hyades
Hydaspes, Hydaspis, *m.,* Hydaspes River

I

iacens, iacentis, fallen, ruined
iacio, iacere, ieci, iactum, (with *fundamenta)* lay foundations
iacto, iactare, iactavi, iactatum, boast about
iactus, iactus, *m.,* throwing, casting, toss
iaculor, iaculari, iaculatus sum, strive after
iaculum, iaculi, *n.,* javelin
iamdudum, *adv.,* for some time
Iapetus, Iapeti, *m.,* Iapetus
Iapyx, Iapygis, *m.,* the wind which blew from Apulia
Icarius, -a, -um, *adj.,* Icarian
idem, eadem, idem, *adj.,* the same; here used adverbially, "likewise"
iecur, iecuris, *n.,* liver (the alleged seat of passion)
ignis, ignis, *m.,* fire
ignosco, ignoscere, ignovi, ignotum, forgive
ilex, ilicis, *f.,* holm-oak, oak tree
Ilia, Iliae, *f.,* poetic name for Rhea Silvia, daughter of Numitor
Ilium, Ili(i), *n.,* Troy
illacrimabilis-illacrimabile, *adj.,* without tears, pitiless
illic, *adv.,* in that place
imago, imaginis, *f.,* shade, ghost, echo
imbellis-imbelle, *adj.,* unfit for war, unwarlike, peaceful
imber, imbris, *m.,* rain
imbuo, imbuere, imbui, imbutum, soak, steep
immeritus, -a, -um, *adj.,* undeserving
immodicus, -a, -um, *adj.,* getting out of hand, excessive, unrestrained
immortalis-immortale, *adj.,* deathless, immortal
imperiosus, -a, -um, *adj.,* bossy, imperious, overpowering
imperium, imperii, *n.,* rule, sway (power over life and death)
impetus, impetus, *m.,* onset
impono, imponere, imposui, impositum, (with dative) place in, place upon, put
impotens, impotentis, *adj.,* not having power over oneself, furious, uncontrollable
imprimo, imprimere, impressi, impressum, press upon, imprint, mark
improbus, -a, -um, *adj.,* bad, shameless, restless, violent, unruly

imus, -a, -um, *adj.,* bottom, below, lowest

Inachus, Inachi, *m,,* Inachus, a mythical first king of Argos

incestus, -a, -um, *adj.,* unclean, impure, guilty

inclamo, inclamare, inclamavi, inclamatum, shout at, scold, chide

incolumis-incolume, *adj.,* unharmed

incorruptus, -a, -um, *adj.,* unspoiled, genuine

incumbo, incumbere, incubui, incubitum, press upon, bear down on

indico, indicare, indicavi, indicatum, show

indocilis-indocile, *adj.,* difficult to be taught

indomitus, -a, -um, *adj.,* unsubdued, invincible

inermis-inerme, *adj.,* unarmed

iners, inertis, *adj.,* lifeless

infamis-infame, *adj.,* ill-famed, infamous

infernus, -a, -um, *adj.,* infernal, of the lower world

infestus, -a, -um, *adj.,* disturbed, dangerous, adverse

inficio, inficere, infeci, infectum, stain, tint

infimus, -a, -um, *adj.,* lowly

infirmus, -a, -um, *adj.,* weak, infirm, sick

informis-informe, *adj.,* hideous, nasty (winter)

infrequens, infrequentis, *adj.,* infrequent

ingens, ingentis, *adj.,* huge, mighty, tall, towering

inhorresco, inhorrescere, inhorrui, rustle

inhospitalis-inhospitale, *adj.,* inhospitable, unfriendly

iniquus, -a, -um, *adj.,* hostile, uneven, dangerous, unfair, harsh

innumerabilis-innumerabile, *adj.,* countless, innumerable

inops, inopis, *adj.,* needy, poor

inquus, -a, -um, *adj.,* unequal, stubborn

inruptus, -a, -um, *adj.,* unbroken, unbreakable

insaniens, insanientis, *adj.,* insane, mad

insero, inserere, inserui, insertum, insert, place among

insignis-insigne, *adj.,* distinguished, renowned

insolens, insolentis, *adj.,* excessive, unusual, unused, unaccustomed

insto, instare, institi, draw near, press closely upon, threaten

intaminatus, -a, -um, *adj.,* uncontaminated, undefiled

integer-integra-integrum, *adj.,* intact, whole, pure, innocent, blameless

intemptatus, -a, -um, *adj.,* untried

interdum, *adv.,* sometimes

intereo, interire, interii, interitum, be lost, perish

interfundo, interfundere, interfudi, interfusum, flow between

interior-interius, *adj.,* inner

interlunium, interluni(i), *n.,* new moon

interpello, interpellare, interrupt (a speaker)

intersum, interesse, interfui, make a difference

intimus, -a, -um, *adj.,* innermost, remotest

intonsus, -a, -um, *adj.,* with uncut hair, i.e., flowing

inutilis-inutile, *adj.,* useless

invicem, *adv.,* in turn

invideo, invidere, invidi, invisum, begrudge, scorn, envy
invidus, -a, -um, *adj.,* envious, jealous
invisus, -a, -um, *adj.,* hated
iocosus, -a, -um, *adj.,* playful, merry
iracundior: *comp. adj.* from *iracundus, -a, -um, adj.,* angry
iracundus, -a, -um, *adj.,* angry, wrathful
Italia, Italiae, *f.,* Italy
Italus, -a, -um, *adj.,* Italian
iter, itineris, *n.,* journey, (with the verb *facio)* travel, route
itero, iterare, iteravi, iteratum, do (a thing) a second time, repeat
Iuba, Iubae, *m.,* Juba, king of Numidia in Africa
iubeo, iubere, iussi, iussum, order, bid
Iudaeus, -a, -um, *adj.,* Jewish; used substantively, "the Jews"
iugum, iugi, *n.,* yoke
iunctus, -a, -um, *adj.,* closed, latched
Iuppiter, Iovis, *m.,* Jupiter; (figuratively) sky
ius, iuris, *n.,* justice, (figuratively) court
iuventa, iuventae, *f.,* youth
iuvo, iuvare, iuvi, iutum, please, delight

L

labor, labi, lapsus sum, slide, glide, slip by, slip away
laboro, laborare, laboravi, laboratum, strive, struggle
labrum, labri, *n.,* lip
lacerta, lacertae, *f.,* lizard
lacertus, lacerti, *m.,* upper arm
laceso, lacessere, lacessivi, lacessitum, provoke
lacrimosus, -a, -um, *adj.,* tearful
laedo, laedere, laesi, laesum, hurt
laetitia, laetitiae, *f.,* joy
laetus, -a, -um, *adj.,* happy, (with ablative of specification) delighting in
Lalage, Lalages, *f.,* Lalage
lambo, lambere, lambi, lick, wash, water
lana, lanae, *f.,* wool; (figuratively) clothing
languidus, -a, -um, *adj.,* sluggish
lapis, lapidis, *m.,* stone, marble
laqueatus, -a, -um, *adj.,* paneled, coffered
large, *adv.,* copiously, generously
lascivus, -a, -um, *adj.,* playful, frolicsome, frisky
latens, latentis, *adj.,* hidden
lateo, latere, latui, lie hidden, remain, obscure
Latona, Latonae, *f.,* Latona, the mother of Apollo and Diana
latus, -a, -um, *adj.,* wide
latus, lateris, *n.,* flank, side; (figuratively) body, section
laurus, lauri, *f.,* laurel, laurel tree
laus, laudis, *f.,* praise

lavo, lavere, lavi, lautum, wash

lenis-lene, *adj.,* soft, gentle, moderately disposed, "kind to the idea of"

lentus, -a, -um, *adj.,* gentle, patient, slow, slow-burning, lingering, sluggish, **leo, leonis,** *m.,* lion

lepus, leporis, *m.,* hare

Lesbous, -a, -um, *adj.,* Lesbian, dealing with the island of Lesbos

Lethaeus, -a, -um, *adj.,* Lethaean, of or belonging to the River Lethe

letum, leti, *n.,* death

Leuconoe, Leuconoes, *f.,* Leuconoe, name of a girl

levior: *comp. adj.,* from *levis-leve, adj.,* light

levis-leve, *adj.,* light-footed, lightly tripping, light, ghostly, polished, smooth

libens, libentis, *adj.,* willing, ready, glad

liber-libera-liberum, *adj.,* free

libero, liberare, liberavi, liberatum, free

libido, libidinis, *f.,* passion, pleasure, lust, sensuality

Libitina, Libitinae, *f.,* Libitina, the goddess of corpses

Liburna, Liburnae, *f.,* a light war vessel

Libycus, -a, -um, *adj.,* Libyan, African

licet, licuit, licitum est, it is allowed, it is permitted

Licinius, Licini(i), *m.,* Licinius, adopted brother of Maecenas' wife, Terentia

lictor, lictoris, *m.,* lictor, attendant who precedes the consul and clears the way

lignum, ligni, *n.,* wood, timber

limen, liminis, *n.,* threshhold

lino, linere, levi, litum, smear, daub, seal

linquo, linquere, liqui, leave behind

linteum, lintei, *n.,* sail

liquidus, -a, -um, *adj.,* flowing, clear, liquid

liquo, liquare, liquavi, liquatum, strain

lis, litis, *f.,* a lawsuit, case

litus, litoris, *n.,* shore

lituus, litui, *m.,* cavalry trumpet

loquax, loquacis, *adj.,* babbling, talkative

loquor, loqui, locutus sum, speak, talk

lucidus, -a, -um, *adj.,* shining

lucrum, lucri, *n.,* gain, profit

luctor, luctari, luctatus sum, wrestle

ludibrium, ludubri(i), *n.,* mockery, plaything

lugubris-lugubre, *adj.,* of mourning

lupus, lupi, *m.,* wolf

Lydia, Lydiae, *f.,* Lydia, the real or fictitious girlfriend of Horace

lympha, lymphae, *f.,* clear water

lymphatus, -a, -um, *adj.,* maddened, intoxicated

lyra, lyrae, *f.,* lyre

M

macero, macerare, maceravi, maceratum, worry, fret, be mentally tortured

macies, maciei, *f.,* disease

Maecenas, Maecenatis, *m.,* Maecenas, friend and patron of Horace

maestus, -a, -um, *adj.,* sad

magis., *adv.,* more (than usual)

male, *adv.,* badly, faintly

malignus, -a, -um, *adj.,* malicious, envious

malobathrum, malobathri, *n.,* perfume

malum, mali, *n.,* evil, problem, trouble

malus, mali, *m.,* mast

mano, manare, manavi, manatum, flow, run

manus, manus, *f.,* hand

Mareoticus, -a, -um, *adj.,* Mareotic (wine)

Marsus, -a, -um, *adj.,* Marsian

mas, maris, *m.,* male

Massicus, -a, -um, *adj.,* Massican; a noted wine from northern Campania

Massicus, Massici, *m.,* Massic, a wine produced in northern Campania

matrona, matronae, *f.,* wife, consort

Maurus, -a, -um, *adj.,* Moorish

mediocritas, mediocritatis, *f.,* moderation

meditor, meditari, meditatus sum, think over, consider

Medus, Medi, *m.,* Mede, Persian, Parthian

Melpomene, Melpomenes, *f.,* Melpomene, the muse of tragedy

membrum, membri, *n.,* body part, limb, body

memini, meminisse, remember

memor, memoris, *adj.,* mindful, remembering

mendax, mendacis, *adj.,* deceiving, deceptive, false, mendacious, deceptive

mens, mentis, *f.,* mind, (level) head

mensa, mensae, *f.,* table

mentum, menti, *n.,* chin

mercator, mercatoris, *m.,* merchant

merces, mercedis, *f.,* wages, reward

Mercurius, Mercuri(i), *m.,* Mercury, messenger of the gods

meritum, meriti, *n.,* achievement, merit

merum, meri, *n.,* unmixed wine

meta, metae, *f.,* a stone turning post in a chariot race

metuo, metuere, metui, fear, be afraid of

metus, metus, *m.,* fear

militaris-militare, *adj.,* warlike, bellicose

militia, militiae, *f.,* military service

Minae, Minarum, *f. pl.,* Threat(s) (a personification)

minax, minacis, *adj.,* threatening, menacing

minister, ministri, *m.,* servant

Minos, Minois, *m.,* Minos, king of Knossos on Crete

minuo, minuere, minui, minutum, lessen, diminish, shrivel

misere, *adv.,* desperately
miseror, miserari, miseratus sum, pity
mitesco, mitescere, grow mild
mobilis-mobile, *adj.,* fickle, mobile, quivering
moderor, moderari, moderatus sum, play, sound
modicus, -a, -um, *adj.,* plain
modo, *adv.,* sometimes
modus, modi, *m.,* limit, measure, meter, (figuratively) poetry
moechus, moechi, *m.,* adulterer
moles, molis, *f.,* mass (of stone), structure
molior, moliri, molitus sum, do with great effort, struggle to build
mollis-molle, *adj.,* gentle
mollius *adv.,* more gracefully
monstrum, monstri, *n.,* monster
monumentum, monumenti, *n.,* a monument, written record, document
mora, morae, *f.,* delay
morbus, morbi, *m.,* disease
morior, mori, mortuus sum, die
moror, morari, moratus sum, (poetic equivalent of *vivo)* live, dwell, linger
morosus, -a, -um, *adj.,* crabby, grumpy
mors, mortis, *f.,* death
mos, moris, *m.,* custom, manner, institution, (in plural) morals, character
moveo, movere, movi, motum, move, touch
mox, *adv.,* soon, (in a series) then, next
mugio, mugire, mugivi, mugitum, bellow
muliebriter, *adv.,* like a woman
multum., *adv.,* much, very
multus, -a, -um, *adj.,* much, (pl.) many
munditia, munditiae, *f.,* cleanliness, elegance
mundus, mundi, *m.,* world
munus, muneris, *n.,* gift, bounty, favor, bribe
murex, muricis, *m.,* purple dye
muto, mutare, mutavi, mutatum, change, exchange, trade
Myrtous, -a, -um, *adj.,* Myrtoan
myrtus, myrti, *f.,* myrtle

N

namque, *conj.,* for
nascor, nasci, natus sum, be born
natalis-natale, *adj.,* natal, (as a substantive) birthplace
nato, natare, natavi, natatum, swim
navita, navitae, *m.,* sailor
nebula, nebulae, *f.,* mist, fog
necessitas, necessitatis, *f.,* fate, destiny, law of nature, necessity
nectar, nectaris, *n.,* the drink of the gods, nectar
necto, nectere, nexi, nexum, weave

nefas, *n.,* (indeclinable) that which is morally wrong or impious

neglectus, -a, -um, *adj.,* outraged, neglected, slighted

nego, negare, negavi, negatum, deny

nemus, nemoris, *n.,* grove

nepos, nepotis, *m.,* grandson

nequiquam, *adv.,* to no avail, in vain

nescio quid, *indef. pron.,* something or other

nescio, nescire, nescivi, nescitum, not to know

nescius, -a, -um, *adj.,* ignorant of, not knowing, unfamiliar with

niger, nigra, nigrum, *adj.,* black, dark, lifeless, gloomy

nil agis: a colloquial expression, "You are doing nothing," "Nothing of the kind!"

nil habeo quod agam = "I have nothing to do"

nimbus, nimbi, *m.,* dark cloud, rain cloud, storm cloud

nimium, *adv.,* excessively, too much

nitens, nitentis, *adj.,* shining, glistening

niteo, nitere, nitui, (with dative) dazzle, glisten

nivalis-nivale, *adj.,* snowy

nix, nivis, *f.,* snow

nobilis-nobile, *adj.,* well-known, famous

noceo, nocere, nocui, (with dative) harm

nomen, nominis, *n.,* reputation, fame

non secus, *adv.,* not otherwise, just as

nosco, noscere, novi, notum, get to know

nota, notae, *f.,* impression, mark, vintage

Notus, Noti, *m.,* the south wind

novus, -a, -um, *adj.,* modern

nubes, nubis, *f.,* cloud

nubilus, -a, -um, *adj.,* cloudy

nudus, -a, -um, *adj.,* nude, stripped

nugae, nugarum, *f. pl.,* trifles, nonsense

numerus, numeri, *m.,* number, (figuratively) astrology.

numquid, *adv.,* (introduces direct question)

nuntius, nunti(i), *m.,* messenger

nuper, *adv.,* lately

nuto, nutare, nutavi, nutatum, nod with the head

nutrix, nutricis, *f.,* nurse

Nympha, Nymphae, *f.,* nymph

O

obeo, obire, obivi (obii), obitum, die

obligo, obligare, obligavi, obligatum, pledge, owe

obliquus, -a, -um, *adj.,* winding

obliviosus, -a, -um, *adj.,* causing forgetfulness

obscurus, -a, -um, *adj.,* lowly

obsoletus, -a, -um, *adj.,* shabby, dilapidated, run-down

obstrepo, obstrepere, obstrepui, obstrepitum, resound, roar

obstringo, obstringere, obstrinxi, obstrictum, bind up, confine

obvius, -a, -um, *adj.,* in the way of

occido, occidere, occidi, occasum, die

occupo, occupare, occupavi, occupatum, seize, break, break in

occurro, occurrere, occurri, occursum, meet, confront

ocior-ocius, *adj.,* swifter

ocius, *adv.,* sooner

odi, odisse, (defective verb) (with an infinitive) disdain (to), be reluctant (to)

odor, odoris, *m.,* scent, perfume

officio, officere, offeci, offectum, (with dative) block, impede, get in the way of **dis, ditis,** *adj.,* wealthy, rich

olim, *adv.,* once, someday

onus, oneris, *n.,* burden

operosiores: *comp. adj.* from *operosus, -a, -um, adj.,* troublesome

oppedo, oppedere, (vulgar) (with dative) break wind in the face of, fart at, insult

oppono, opponere, opposui, oppositum, offer, oppose

opus est: an idiom meaning "there is need of" (with ablative)

ora, orae, *f.,* shore

Orcus, Orci, *m.,* Orcus, god of the lower world

ordino, ordinare, ordinavi, ordinatum, arrange

orior, oriri, ortus sum, arise, rise, stir, get up

orno, ornare, ornavi, ornatum, decorate, adorn

ornus, orni, *f.,* mountain ash (tree)

Ornytus, Ornyti, *m.,* Ornytus, father of Calais

Orpheus, Orphei, *m.,* the poet Orpheus

osculum, osculi, *n.,* little mouth, kiss

otium, oti(i), *n.,* leisure time, as opposed to business time *negotium*

otium, oti(i), *n.,* peace, tranquility

P

palaestra, palaestrae, *f.,* a place for wrestling

palma, palmae, *f.,* palm branch

par, paris, *adj.,* equal

Parca, Parcae, *f.,* Fate, goddess of fate

parcius: *comp. adv.,* from *parcus, -a, -um, adj.,* sparing, less often

parco, parcere, peperci, parsum, (with dative) spare, refrain from

parcus, -a, -um, *adj.,* sparing, stingy

parens, parentis, *m.,* author, inventor

paries, parietis, *f.,* wall (interior)

parmula, parmulae, *f.,* shield

Parthi, Parthorum, *m. pl.,* the Parthians, a people in central Asia Minor

parvus, -a, -um, *adj.,* little; (used substantively) "a little"

patens, patentis, *adj.,* open

pateo, patere, patui, stand open, lie open

paternus, -a, -um, *adj.,* ancestral, native

patientia, patientiae, *f.,* endurance, patience, resignation

patior, pati, passus sum, allow, permit, experience, suffer, undergo
patrius, -a, -um., *adj.,* of your country
pauper, pauperis, *adj.,* (with genitive) poor (in)
pauperies, pauperiei, *f.,* poverty
paveo, pavere, pavi, quake with fear, tremble
pavidus, -a, -um, *adj.,* frightened, terrified, panicky, fearful
pavimentum, pavimenti, *n.,* pavement
pectus, pectoris, *n.,* chest, heart
pecus, pecoris, *n.,* flock
pelagus, pelagi, *n.,* sea
penitus, *adv.,* deeply, dearly, from the bottom of the heart, deep down, within
penna, pennae, *f.,* feather, wing
per festos dies = throughout the holidays
perdo, perdere, perdidi, perditum, destroy, do away with, waste
perennius: *comp. adv.* from *perennis-perenne, adj.,* lasting, enduring
pereo, perire, perii or perivi, periturus, die, perish
perfundo, perfundere, perfudi, perfusum, steep, drench, douse
Perithous, Perithoi, *m.,* Perithous, friend of Theseus
permisceo, permiscere, permiscui, permixtum, mix, blend
permitto, permittere, permisi, permissum, entrust
permuto, permutare, permutavi, permutatum, change completely
perpetior, perpeti, perpessus sum, endure
perrumpo, perrumpere, perrupi, perruptum, break through
Persae, Persarum, *m. pl.,* the Persians (Parthians), people of the Far East
persequor, persequi, persecutus sum, persistently pursue
Persicus, -a, -um, *adj.,* Persian, oriental
pertinax, pertinacis, *adj.,* tenacious, unyielding, resisting
pestis, pestis, *f.,* disease, plague
petitor, petitoris, *m.,* candidate
pharetra, pharetrae, *f.,* quiver
phaselus, phaseli, *m.,* skiff, boat
Philippi, Philipporum, *m. pl.,* a city in Thrace
philyra, philyrae, *f.,* linden bark
Phrygius, -a, -um, *adj.,* Phrygian, Trojan
pictus, -a, -um, *adj.,* painted
pietas, pietatis, *f.,* loyalty, righteousness, devotion (to gods and fellow man)
piger-pigra-pigrum, *adj.,* lifeless, barren, sluggish, slow, lazy
pignus, pignoris, *n.,* pledge, ring or bracelet
pinus, pini, *f.,* pine (a dark, massive tree)
piscis, piscis, *m.,* fish
pius, -a, -um, *adj.,* devoted, pious, loyal
placeo, placere, placui, placitum, please
placo, placare, placavi, placatum, appease, please
plaga, plagae, *f.,* net
plausus, plausus, *m.,* applause
plerumque, *adv.,* generally, usually, for the most part

plus, pluris, *adj.,* more

Pluto, Plutonis, *m.,* Pluto, king of the underworld

poculum, poculi, *n.,* cup

podagra, podagrae, *f.,* arthritis in the foot

Poena, Poenae, *f.,* Vengeance, Retribution, goddess of punishment

pomifer-pomifera-pomiferum, *adj.,* bountiful, fruitful

Pompeius, Pompei(i), *m.,* Pompey, comrade-in-arms of Horace at Philippi

pono, ponere, posui, positum, place down, put down, calm

Ponticus, -a, -um, *adj.,* of Pontus

pontifex, pontificis, *m.,* high priest

poples, poplitis, *m.,* hollow of the knee, knee

popularis-populare, *adj.,* favoring the people, the people's

populus, populi, *f.,* poplar

porrigo, porrigere, porrexi, porrectum, offer

portentum, portenti, *n.,* monster

portus, portus, *m.,* port

posco, poscere, poscui, poscitum, ask, ask back

post, *prep.,* behind

posterus, -a, -um, *adj.,* future, of posterity, next, following, ensuing

postis, postis *m.,* doorpost, (figuratively) door

Postumus, Postumi, *m.,* Postumus, a man's name

potens, potentis, *adj.,* powerful, influential

potior, potiri, potitus sum, (with ablative) gain possession of, become master of

potior-potius, *adj.,* better, rather/more preferable, superior, more favored

poto, potare, potavi, potatum, drink

praebeo, praebere, praebui, praebitum, hold out, offer

praecedo, praecedere, praecessi, praecessum, go in front, lead the way

praeceps, praecipitis, *adj.,* headfirst, stormy

praecipio, praecipere, praecepi, praeceptum, teach

praesens, praesentis, *adj.,* present

praesidium, praesidi(i), *n.,* protection, protector

praeter, *prep.,* (with accusative) except

praetereo, praeterire, praeterivi or **praeterii, praeteritum,** go/pass by, flow within

precor, precari, precatus sum, pray, beg

prelum, preli, *n.,* a winepress

premo, premere, pressi, pressum, bear down upon, stay close to, overwhelm, catch

prenso, prensare, prensavi, prensatum, grasp, clutch at

prex, precis, *f.,* prayer (more common in the plural)

Priamus, Priami, *m.,* Priam, king of Troy

primus, -a, -um, *adj.,* first

princeps, principis, *m.,* first man, most distinguished man, leader

priscus, -a, -um, *adj.,* ancient, original, pure, first

prius, *adv.,* earlier, in the past, previously

privatus, -a, -um, *adj.,* of or belonging to a private individual, civilian

procella, procellae, *f.,* gale, squall, storm

proditor, proditoris, *m.,* traitor, betrayer

profanus, -a, -um, *adj.,* before the temple, not sacred, common

promineo, prominere, prominui, stand out
promo, promere, prompsi, promptum, bring before the world, exalt
propero, properare, properavi, properatum, hasten, rush
propinquus, -a, -um, *adj.,* near
proprius, -a, -um, *adj.,* one's own
prospicio, prospicere, prospexi, prospectum, look into the distance at
protero, protere, protrivi, protritum, tread upon, tred on the heels of
protervus, -a, -um, *adj.,* shameless, rowdy
prudens, prudentis, *adj.,* wise, prudent
pubes, pubis, *f.,* youth
pudicus, -a, -um, *adj.,* chaste
Pudor, Pudoris, *m.,* modesty (personification)
pudor, pudoris, *m.,* sense of propriety, restraint
puer, pueri, *m.,* slave (whether young or old)
pulchre, *adv.,* beautifully, fully, splendidly, very well
pullus, -a, -um, *adj.,* dark (green), seasoned
pulso, pulsare, pulsavi, pulsatum, beat, strike (in the dance)
pulvinar, pulvinaris, *n.,* couch
pulvis, pulveris, *m.,* dust
pumex, pumicis, *m.,* soft rock, pumice
puppis, puppis, *f.,* stern of a vessel
purior: *comp. adj.* from *purus, -a, -um, adj.,* pure, innocent
purpura, purpurae, *f.,* purple garment, splendid clothing
purus, -a, -um, *adj.,* clean, wholesome, pure
pyramis, pyramidis, *f.,* pyramid
Pyrrha, Pyrrhae, *f.,* Pyrrha

Q

quadrigae, quadrigarum, *f. pl.,* chariot
quadrimus, -a, -um, *adj.,* four-year-old
quaero, quaerere, quaesivi, quaesitum, gain, win, look for, seek, search for
qualis-quale, *adj.,* of what sort or kind
quam, *adv.,* (with a superlative degree) as … as possible, how
quamquam, *conj.,* although
quamvis, *conj.,* although
quandocumque, *adv.,* at some time or other
quare, *interrogative adv.,* why
quarta pars, quartae partis, *f.,* one fourth
quatio, quatere, (no perfect active), **quassum,** shake, beat, strike, shatter
querimonia, quaerimoniae, *f.,* difference of opinion, complaint
questus, questus, *m.,* complaint
quia, *conj.,* because (of the fact that), the fact that
quid agis: a conventional greeting, "How are you?"
quid, *adv.,* why, how
quidam, quaedam, quiddam, *indef. pron.,* a certain person, someone
quilibet, quaelibet, quidlibet, *pron.,* anyone, anything

quin et, *adv.,* furthermore
Quintilius, Quintili(i), *m.,* Quintilius Varus, a friend of Vergil and of Horace
quintus, -a, -um, *adj.,* a fifth
Quiris, Quiritis, *m.,* a Roman citizen
quis-quid, *inter. adj.,* which, what
quislibet-quidlibet, *indef. pron.,* anything
quisquae-quaeque-quidque, *interog. adj.,* whichever
quisquam, cuiusquam, *pron.,* anyone, anybody
quisquis-quidquid, *pron.,* whoever
quo tendis?: "Where are you headed?"
quo, *adv.,* (indicating direction) where, to where, to the place where, why
quodsi, *conj.,* but if
quondam, *adv.,* (a rare meaning) sometimes
quotquot, (indeclinable) *adj.,* however many

R

rabies, rabiei, *f.,* fury, rage
ramus, rami, *m.,* branch
rapax-rapacis, *adj.,* rapacious; (with adverbial force) "swiftly"
rapio, rapere, rapui, raptum, rush on, make (the day) rush by, snatch, drag
raro, *adv.,* rarely
ratis, ratis, *f.,* boat, ship
raucus, -a, -um, *adj.,* coarse, rough
recens, recentis, *adj.,* recent, recently created, fresh
recipio, recipere, recepi, receptum, regain
reclinatus, -a, -um, *adj.,* reclining, having reclined
recludo, recludere, reclusi, reclusum, reveal, open, disclose
recreo, recreare, recreavi, recreatum, refresh, revive
rectius: *comp. adv.* from *rectus, -a, -um, adj.,* upright, correct, proper
recurro, recurrere, recurri, recursum, return
reddo, reddere, reddidi, redditum, return, render, give in return
redemptor, -oris, *m.,* contractor
redeo, redire, redii, reditum, return
redigo, redigere, redegi, redactum, restore (to a former situation)
redono, redonare, redonavi, redonatum, restore
refero, referre, retuli, relatum, carry back
reficio, reficere, refeci, refectum, repair
regalis-regale, *adj.,* royal, regal
regia, regiae, *f.,* palace
regius, -a, -um, *adj.,* royal, of royal blood
rego, regere, rexi, rectum, guide
reicio, reicere, reieci, reiectum, reject
religio, religionis, *f.,* religious awe, conscience, scruple
religo, religare, religavi, religatum, tie back
relinquo, relinquere, reliqui, relictum, leave, abandon
remigium, remigi(i), *n.,* rowing, (figuratively) oars

remotus, -a, -um, *adj.,* secluded

remus, remi, *m.,* oar, (figuratively) galley

reor, reri, ratus sum, think

reparo, reparare, reparavi, reparatum, repair, restore, seek

repeto, repetere, repetivi, repetitum, return to, recollect

repono, reponere, reposui, repositum, conduct, replenish, pile

repulsa, repulsae, *f.,* defeat

res, rei, *f.,* circumstances, (financial) resources, situation

reseco, resecare, resecui, resectum, prune, cut back

resorbeo, resorbere, pull back, draw back (in)

respondeo, respondere, respondi, responsum, answer a summons, appear in court

restituo, restituere, restitui, restitutum, restore (to life)

resto, restare, restiti, survive, remain

retrorsum, *adv.,* backwards

rideo, ridere, risi, risum, smile, laugh

ripa, ripae, *f.,* bank of a river

risus, -us, *m.,* laughter, smile

ritus, ritus, *m.,* rite, style, fashion

rivus, rivi, *m.,* course, channel, stream, brook

rixa, rixae, *f.,* quarrel, fight

robur, roboris, *n.,* oak

robustus, -a, -um, *adj.,* hardened (by)

rosa, rosae, *f.,* rose

roseus, -a, -um, *adj.,* rosy, rose colored, pink

rota, rotae, *f.,* wheel

ruber-rubra-rubrum, *adj.,* red

rubus, rubi, *m.,* bramble

rudis-rude, *adj.,* (with genitive) untrained in, unskilled in

ruga, rugae, *f.,* wrinkle

ruina, ruinae, *f.,* ruin

rumpo, rumpere, rupi, ruptum, break

ruo, ruere, rui, rush

rursus, *adv.,* again

rus, ruris, *n.,* fields, country estate

S

sabbata, sabbatorum, *n. pl.,* the Jewish sabbath

Sabellus, -a, -um, *adj.,* Sabine

Sabinum, Sabini, *n.,* a cheap, local wine, Sabine wine

Sabinus, -a, -um, *adj.,* of or belonging to Sabine country

sacrum, sacri, *n.,* sacred rite

saepe, *adv.,* often

saepius, *adv.,* more often

saevio, saevire, saevii, saevitum, rage, rave

saevus, -a, -um, *adj.,* cruel, savage, hostile

Saliaris-Saliare, *adj.,* of the Salii, priests of Mars

salinum, salini, *n.,* salt shaker

salsus, -a, -um, *adj.,* witty, funny

saltus, saltus, *m.,* mountain pasture

salvus, -a, -um, *adj.,* safe, unhurt, well

sanius: *comp. adv.,* from *sanus, -a, -um, adj.,* sane, sensible

sapienter, *adv.,* wisely

sapientia, sapientiae, *f.,* philosophy

sapio, sapere, sapivi or **sapii,** be discerning, be wise, have good taste

sapor, saporis, *m.,* taste, sense of taste

sarculum, sarculi, *n.,* hoe

satis, *adv.,* enough

Satyrus, Satyri, *m.,* Satyr, a forest deity with goat's feet

saucius, -a, -um, *adj.,* injured, battered

scando, scandere, scandi, scansum, board, climb

scelestus, -a, -um, *adj.,* wicked, criminal

scelus, sceleris, *n.,* sin, crime

scilicet, *adv.,* assuredly, of course, certainly

scio, scire, scivi, scitum, know, understand, know how to use

scopulus, scopuli, *m.,* cliff, rock

secerno, secernere, secrevi, secretum, set apart

seco, secare, secui, sectum, cut

sector, sectari, sectatus sum, seek eagerly

secundus, -a, -um, *adj.,* favorable, prosperous, secondary

securis, securis, *m., f.,* ax, the fasces, a bundle of rods and an ax tied together

sedulus, -a, -um, *adj.,* attentive to detail

semel, *adv.,* once

semotus, -a, -um, *adj.,* distant

senectus, senectutis, *f.,* old age

sentio, sentire, sensi, sensum, experience

serenus, -a, -um, *adj.,* serene

series, seriei, *f.,* series

serius, *adv.* , later

serpens, serpentis, *f.,* snake

serus, -a, -um, *adj.,* late

servo, servare, servavi, servatum, guard, protect, keep

seu ... seu, whether ... or

seu or **sive,** *conj.,* or if

si bene me novi: colloquial expression meaning "if I know me"

si me amas: colloquial expression for "please."

sic (se res) habet: that's the situation

siccus, -a, -um, dry

Siculus, -a, -um, *adj.,* of or belonging to Sicily, Sicilian

sicut, *conj.,* as, just as

sidus, sideris, *n.,* constellation, star

similis-simile, *adj.,* (with dative) similar to

simplex, simplicis, *adj.,* plain, uncluttered, simple

simul = simul ac = simula atque, *conj.,* as soon as

simul ac = as soon as

simul atque, *conj.,* as soon as

Sisyphus, Sisyphi, *m.,* Sisyphus, the king of Corinth

situs, situs, *m.,* structure

sobrius, -a, -um, *adj.,* prudent

sodalis, sodalis, *m.,* companion, comrade

sodes = si audes (uncontracted form), "if you please me," "please"

sol, solis, *m.,* sun

solido...de die, the "solid" day, the business day, the entire day

sollicito, sollicitare, sollicitavi, sollicitatum, disturb, upset

sollicitus, -a, -um, *adj.,* anxious, solicitous

solum, soli, *n.,* ground

solus, -a, -um, *adj.,* deserted

solvo, solvere, solvi, solutum, part, separate, unfasten

somnus, somni, *m.,* sleep

sonitus, sonitus, *m.,* sound

sopor, soporis, *m.,* a deep sleep of death

Soracte, Soractis, *n.,* Soracte, a mountain near Horace's villa

sordes, sordis, *f.,* dirt, filth

sordidus, -a, -um, *adj.,* foul, unclean, disgraceful, vulgar

soror, sororis, *f.,* sister

sors, sortis, *f.,* lot

sortior, sortiri, sortitus sum, assign by lot, obtain by lot, decide the fate of

sospes, sospitis, *adj.,* safe

spatium, spati(i), *n.,* span (of life)

sperno, spernere, sprevi, spretum, scorn, reject, pass up

spero, sperare, speravi, speratum, hope for, expect

spiritus, spiritus, *m.,* breath, inspiration

splendeo, splendere, shine

splendidus, -a, -um, *adj.,* sparkling, glittering, brilliant, stately, august

sponsus, sponsi, *m.,* fiancé

sterno, sternere, stravi, stratum, calm, still, spread, stretch

stridor, -oris, *m.,* noise, whirring

stultitia, stultitiae, *f.,* stupidity

Styx, Stygis, *f.,* the Styx, a river of the underworld

suaviter, *adv.,* very well

sub arta vite = under a grape arbor

sub, *prep.,* (with accussative), during, in the course of

subeo, subire, subii or subivi, subitum, (with ablative of means) go under

onus, oneris, *n.,* burden, load, weight

sublimis-sublime, *adj.,* lofty, towering high, raised up, held high

submoveo, submovere, submovi, submotum, put out of the way, drive off

iste-ista-istud, *adj.,* that (with a pejorative connotation)

suboles, subolis, *f.,* offspring

sudor, sudoris, *m.,* sweat

sulcus, sulci, *m.,* a furrow
summa, summae, *f.,* sum
summoveo, summovere, summovi, summotum, banish, move away
summus, -a, -um, *adj.,* top, highest
sumo, sumere, sumpsi, sumptum, take, assume
superbia, superbiae, *f.,* pride, proud honor
superbus, -a, -um, *adj.,* proud, haughty
supercilium, supercili(i), *n.,* eyebrow
superstes, superstitis, *adj.,* surviving, outliving
superus, -a, -um, *adj.,* high above
supremus, -a, -um, *adj.,* final, last; *suprema die* = death
surgo, surgere, surrexi, surrectum, rise into view, emerge beyond horizon
suscito, suscitare, suscitavi, suscitatum, wake, awake
suspendo, suspendere, suspendi, suspensum, hang up
suspiro, suspirare, suspiravi, suspiratum, sigh
sustineo, sustinere, sustinui, sustentum, hold up, support, sustain, bear
susurrus, susurri, *m.,* whisper
suus, -a, -um, *adj.,* her/his/its own
Syrtis, Syrtis, *f.,* shifting sands of North Africa's coast

T

tabula, tabulae, *f.,* tablet, picture
taceo, tacere, tacui, tacitum, be silent
taedium, taedi(i), *n.,* weariness
Taenarus, Taenari, *m.,* Cape Taenarus
talus, tali, *m.,* the anklebone, ankle; *ad imos talos,* "to my very ankles"
tandem, *adv.,* finally, once and for all
tango, tangere, tetigi, tactum, touch
tantum modo, *adv.,* merely, only, just
tardus, -a, -um, *adj.,* slow, crippling
taurus, tauri, *m.,* bull, ox
tectum, tecti, *n.,* roof, (by synecdoche) house
Telephus, Telephi, *m.,* Telephus, a king of Mysia, son of Heracles and Auge
tellus, telluris, *f.,* land, earth
Tempe, *n. pl.,* (indeclinable) Tempe, a valley in northern Greece
tempero, temperare, temperavi, temperatum, restrain from, refrain from
tempestivus, -a, -um, *adj.,* timely, seasonable, age for
tempora quaerere, look for opportunities, bide one's time
tendo, tendere, tetendi, tensum, stretch
tene = te +ne; ne is the suffix indicating a question
tenebrae, tenebrarum, *f. pl.,* darkness
tener-tenera-tenerum, *adj.,* young, weak, tender
tenuis-tenue, *adj.,* modest, frugal, slight
teres, teretis, *adj.,* thick, close meshed
tergeminus, -a, -um, *adj.,* triple
tergum, tergi, *n.,* back

terminus, termini, *m.,* boundary, limit of property

terreo, terrere, terrui, territum, frighten

testa, testae, *f.,* jar

Thaliarchus, Thaliarchi, *m.,* Thaliarchus

theatrum, theatri, *n.,* theater

Theseus, Thesei, *m.,* Theseus, king of Athens

Thessalus, -a, -um, *adj.,* Thessalian, the country of northern Greece

Thrace, Thraces, *f.,* Thrace, east of Macedonia in northern Greece

Thracius, -a, -um, *adj.,* Thracian, from Thrace

Thraessus, -a, -um, *adj.,* Thracian

Threicius, -a, -um, *adj.,* Thracian

Thurinus, -a, -um, *adj.,* belonging to Thurii, a city of Lucania

tibia, tibiae, *f.,* flute

tigris, tigris, *f.,* tiger

timidus, -a, -um, *adj.,* timid

Timor, Timoris, *m.,* Fear (a personification)

timor, timoris, *m.,* fear

tinguo, tinguere, tinxi, tinctum, stain

tinguo, tinguere, tinxi, tinctus, dye

Tithonus, Tithoni, *m.,* Tithonus, husband of Aurora

Tityos, Tityi, *m.,* Tityos, the giant who was punished in Hades

tollo, tollere, sustuli, sublatum, bear off, carry away, elevate, raise, extol

tono, tonare, tonui, tonitum, thunder

Torquatus, Torquati, *m.,* Torquatus Manlius, a member of the gens Manlia

torreo, torrere, torrui, tostum, burn, scorch, dry up

totidem, indeclinable *adj.* just as many

totus, a, -um, *adj.,* whole, entire

trabs or trabes, trabis, *f.,* rafter, (figuratively) roof; beam, (figuratively) ship

tracto, tractare, tractavi, tractatum, handle

trado, tradere, tradidi, traditum, introduce

transilio, transilire, transilui, leap over, skim across

treceni-ae-a, *adj.,* three-hundred at a time

tremo, tremere, tremui, tremble, shake, quiver

trepido, trepidare, trepidavi, trepidatum, rush along

trepidus, -a, -um, *adj.,* hazardous, stirring

tribuo, tribuere, tribui, tributum, allot, bestow, give

trice(n)simus, -a, -um, *adj.,* thirtieth

triplex, triplicis, *adj.,* three-ply

triremis-trireme, *adj.,* a ship with three banks of oars on each side, a trireme

tristis-triste, *adj.,* sad, gloomy, rainy

triumphus, triumphi, *m.,* triumph

trivium, trivi(i), *n.,* meeting place of three roads, intersection

trux, trucis, *adj.,* fierce, angry (sea)

tuba, tubae, *f.,* infantry trumpet

Tullus, Tulli, *m.,* Tullus Hostilius, the third king of Rome

tumeo, tumere, tumui, swell

tumultuosus, -a, -um, *adj.,* full of uproar, noisy, stormy
tumultus, tumultus, *m.,* tumult, turmoil, headache
turba clientium, the crowd of clients
turba, tubae, *f.,* throng, crowd
turgidus, -a, -um, *adj.,* swollen
turma, turmae, *f.,* troop, squadron
turpis-turpe, *adj.,* filthy, foul, disgusting, ignoble
turpo, turpare, turpavi, turpatum, disfigure, scar (i.e., made black and blue)
turris, turris, *f.,* tower
tussis, tussis, *f.,* cough
tutus, -a, -um, *adj.,* safe, sure
Tyrrhenus, -a, -um, *adj.,* Etruscan

U

udus, -a, -um, *adj.,* moist, damp, humid, pliant
ulcerosus, -a, -um, *adj.,* full of sores, ulcerous
ultimus, -a, -um, *adj.,* extreme
ultra, *adv.,* beyond
ultra, *prep.,* (with accusative) beyond
umbra, umbrae, *f.,* shade, shadow
umbrosus, -a, -um, *adj.,* shadowy, shady
umerus, umeri, *m.,* shoulder
umor, umoris, *m.,* moistness, a liquid, moist tear(s)
unda, undae, *f.,* wave
undique, *adv.,* on all sides, from every quarter
unguentum, unguenti, *n.,* perfume
unus multorum: "one of the many," "one of the ordinary crowd"
urgeo, urgere, ursi, lie heavy on, weigh down, lower, brood, press upon
urna, urnae, *f.,* urn
uro, urere, ussi, ustum, burn, burn up, destroy by fire
usque, *adv.,* all the way
usus, usus, *m.,* use of, wearing of
ut, an exclamatory *adv.,* how, how much better
ut, *conj.,* how
utor, uti, usus sum, (with the ablative) use, make use of
utrimque, *adv.,* on both sides
uva, uvae, *f.,* grape, juice of grapes
uvidus, -a, -um, *adj.,* wet
uxor, uxoris, *f.,* wife

V

vacca, vaccae, *f.,* cow
vacuus, -a, -um, *adj.,* unattached, detached, available
vador, vadari, vadatus sum, put up bail
vadum, vadi, *n.,* sea

vae, *interj.,* ah! alas!

vagor, vagari, vagatus sum, wander

vagus, -a, -um, *adj.,* wandering

valeo, valere, valui, have power, be well, be strong

vallis, vallis, *f.,* valley

vanus, -a, -um, *adj.,* groundless, empty, unsubstantial, shadowy

Varius, Vari(i), *m.,* Varius (an unknown friend of Horace)

vates, vatis, *m.,* poet

Vaticanus, -a, -um, *adj.,* the Vatican hill, west of the Tiber

vello, vellere, velli or **vulsi, vulsum,** pull at, tug at

velum, veli, *n.,* sail

velut, *conj.,* just as

venalis-venale, *adj.,* able to be bought

venator, venatoris, *m.,* hunter

venenatus, -a, -um, *adj.,* poisoned

venenum, veneni, *n.,* poison

ventum erat: (impersonal) "We arrived"

ver, veris, *n.,* spring

verbero, verberare, verberavi, verberatum, batter, beat

veritas, veritatis, *f.,* truth

verro, verrere, verri, versum, sweep

verso, versare, versavi, versatum, turn, shake up

vertex, verticis, *m.,* the top of the head, head

verus, -a, -um, *adj.,* genuine

vescor, vesci, (with ablative) eat, fill oneself with, live on

vestimentum, vestimenti, *n.,* garment, clothing

vestio, vestire, vestivi, vestitum, clothe

veto, vetare, vetui, vetitum, forbid

vexo, vexare, vexavi, vexatum, harass

vicis: *vicem* (accusative singular), *vice* (ablative singular), *f.,* succession

vicus, vici, *m.,* street

viduus, -a, -um, *adj.,* (with ablative) deprived of

vigeo, vigere, vigui, thrive, flourish

vilis-vile, *adj.,* cheap

vin = visne

vinculum, vinculi, *n.,* chain

vinea, vineae, *f.,* vineyard

violens, violentis, *adj.,* violent, wild, raging

virens, virentis, *adj.,* fresh, vigorous, flourishing

vireo, virere, virui, be fresh, be green, flourish, be full of youthful vigor

virga, virgae, *f.,* the magic wand, *caduceus* used by Mercury

viridis-viride, *adj.,* green, fresh

Virtus, Virtutis, *f.,* personification of courage

virtus, virtutis, *f.,* courage, valor

Viscus, Visci, *m.,* Viscus (an unknown friend of Horace)

viso, visere, visi, visum, look at with attention, view, visit, call on

vitiosus, -a, -um, *adj.,* corrupt, bad

vitis, vitis, *f.,* vine, vine branch; (figuratively) wine

vito, vitare, vitavi, vitatum, avoid, shun

vitrum, vitri, *n.,* glass

vivo, vivere, vixi, victum, live; (impersonal usage) "it is lived," "one lives."

vix, *adv.,* scarcely

voco, vocare, vocavi, vocatum, call upon

volgus, volgi, *n.,* masses, multitude, crowd

volo, velle, volui, wish, want, be willing to

volo, volare, volavi, volatum, flit, fly, rush

volucer-volucris-volucre, *adj.,* swift

vomer, vomeris, *m.,* ploughshare, (figuratively) plow

votivus, -a, -um, *adj.,* votive, belonging to a vow, promised by a vow

vox, vocis, *f.,* voice, speech language

vulgaris-vulgare, *adj.,* common

vulgo, vulgare, vulgavi, vulgatum, divulge

vulgus, vulgi, *n.,* crowd

vultus, vultus, *m.,* expression (in the face)

Z

Zephyrus, Zephyri, m., west wind